A GRIMOIRE OF TH
Volume 1. Psalms 1-50

Dr. Lazarus Corbeaux
2019

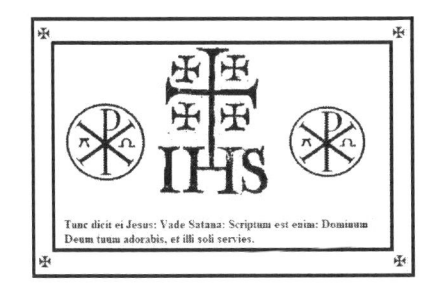

COPYRIGHT & DISCLAIMER

A Grimoire of the Psalms Volume 1. Psalms 1-50
© 2019 Laci Metheny
No part of this book may be reproduced in any written, electronic, recording, or photocopying without the written permission of the author.

This book is not intended as a substitute for medical, legal, or any other professional advice. The reader should regularly consult a physician in regards to the matter of his/her health and particularly in regards to any symptoms that may require diagnosis and medical attention. The reader should also consult licensed legal professionals in regards to any matters of the law, whether criminal or civil. Neither the author nor the publishers assume any liability for the use, or misuse, of any of the information provided in this text. It is presented as an academic study of folklore, and neither the author nor the publisher will assume any liability for damages of any kind, that may result from the use of the information presented here.

CONTACT

Facebook:
http://www.facebook.com/drcorbeauxsconjureroom

Wordpress:
http://www.drcorbeaux.wordpress.com

Youtube:
http://www.youtube.com/user/thetoadsbool

Email: drcorbeaux@gmail.com

+BMN+ATD+OFYL+
Amen
+++
I
N
R
I
I N R I + I N R I
I
N
R
I

INRI✠OW✠C✠T✠B✠SB✠W✠IHVH

A NOTE ON THE TEXT

The order of the Psalms will be based upon the King James Version of the Bible, as it is the most widespread, so to use this text you will need either a KJV Bible or one of the small New Testaments that contain the Book of Psalms.

The Psalm number will be presented in the left hand corner, followed by the specific seals, talismans, and workings that relate to that Psalm.

> May God bless you in your work,
> Dr. Lazarus Corbeaux
> +++

PSALM 1

PROTECTION FROM UNGODLY PEOPLE

THE LORD KNOWETH THE
WAY OF THE RIGHTEOUS

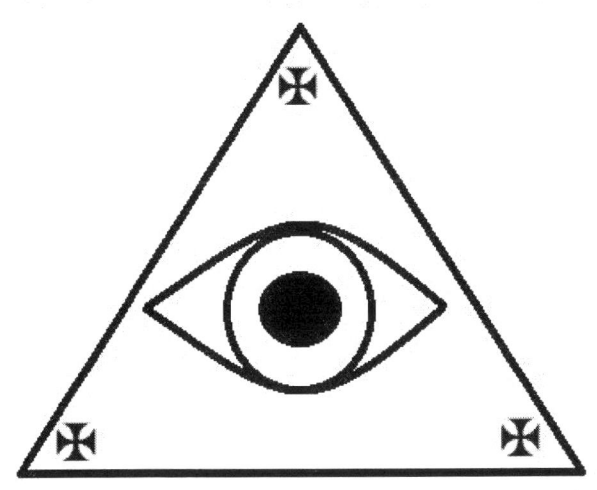

but the way of the ungodly shall perish ✠✠✠

Mark the above talisman in red ink and recite Psalm 1 over it for nine days. After the 9 days, fold the corners, so the crosses cover the center of the eye and sew the talisman up into a piece of purple cloth with a small piece of a broken mirror. Wear this around the neck from a cotton string.

FOR SAFE PREGNANCY

```
        ✠
    SANCTUS  ╱╲  SANCTUS
           ╱    ╲
          ╱      ╲
     ✠ ╱ DOMINUS DEUS ╲ ✠
          ╲      ╱
           ╲    ╱
            ╲  ╱
             ✠
          SANCTUS
```

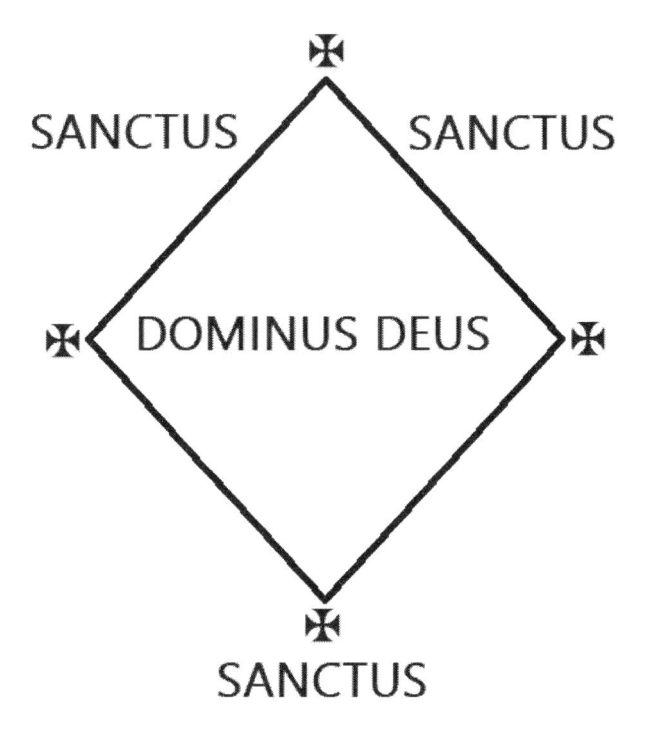

Take some red ink and pray Psalm 1 over it three times. A permanent red marker will also work. Then draw the above image on a piece of white cloth, such as a handkerchief. Carry this handkerchief to three Sunday Masses and give it to the pregnant woman to wear under her shirt against her abdomen.

PSALM 2

TO DISEMPOWER AN ENEMY

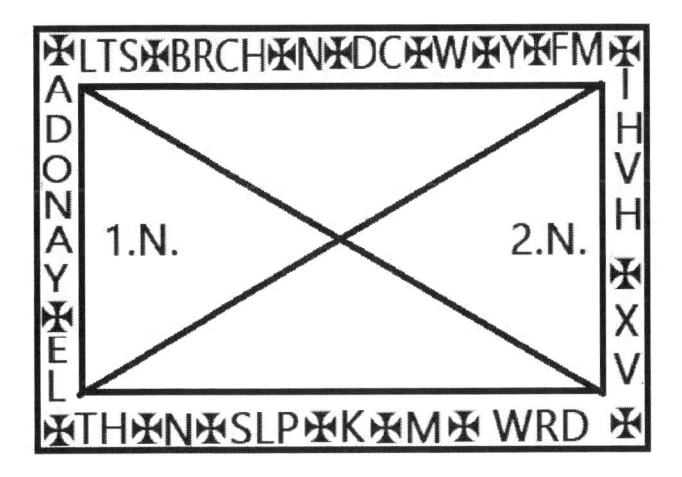

```
✠LTS✠BRCH✠N✠DC✠W✠Y✠FM✠
A                          I
D                          H
O                          V
N      1.N.      2.N.      H
A                          ✠
Y                          X
✠                          V
E
L
✠TH✠N✠SLP✠K✠M✠ WRD ✠
```

Copy the above seal and on 1.N write your enemy's first name; and on 2.N write your enemy's last name.

On a Saturday during the Hour of Saturn, copy the seal as instructed in black ink, or if you are able, on a sheet of lead.

Set three black candles to burn around the seal and recite the psalm 15 times.

After the candles have burned out, roll the seal away from you and drive a pin through it if it is made of paper; or an iron nail if you are using a lead sheet.

Bury the seal in the west side of a cemetery.

TO MAKE YOUR ENEMIES FEAR YOU

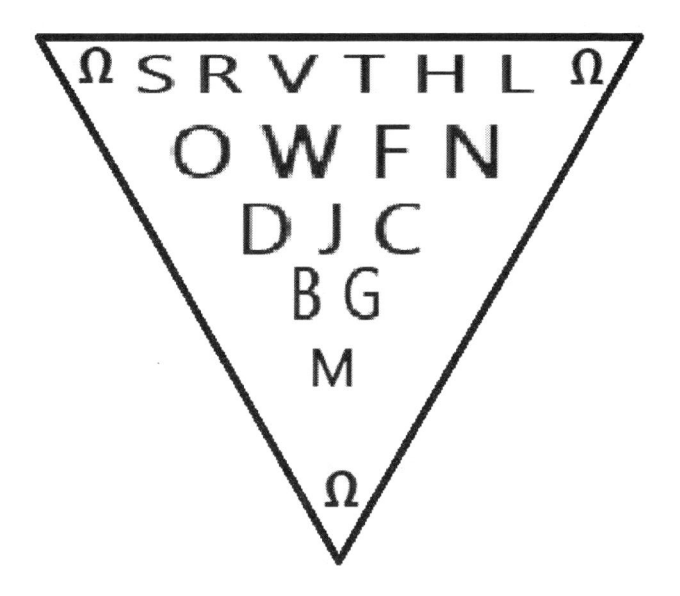

```
Ω S R V T H L Ω
  O W F N
   D J C
    B G
     M
     Ω
```

Engrave the above on a piece of iron in the day and hour of Mars, the moon increasing. Fumigate it with dragon's blood while reciting the psalm 5 times. It can be worn as a talisman; or the enchanted iron dipped in stormwater five times, then sprinkled on your target's lawn, or the water introduced to their food.

TO OUTSHINE YOUR COMPETITION

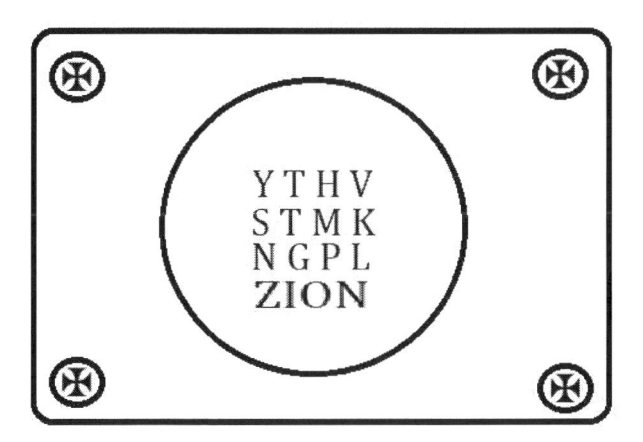

```
Y T H V
S T M K
N G P L
ZION
```

Draw out the following on the center of a new white plate in gold paint or ink. Set 4 gold candles on top of the crosses in the diagram and recite the psalm 4 times; once each time you light the candle. After the candles are lit, pray and meditate on the matter you are working towards, and implore the Lord's help.

After the candles have burned out, regularly place some water in the plate and pray the Lord's prayer four times. Pour the water from the plate over your head while facing the east.

PSALM 3

For Headache, Backache, or bodily pains

1. Recite the psalm three times over the injured part.
2. Write the psalm on clean paper, burn it to ashes, and mix the ashes with olive oil. Mark three crosses on the affected part.
3. Mark the following on clean paper and carry in the shoe to prevent cramps

```
✠ PHLFBP ✠
  Ω Ω Ω Ω
   Ω Ω Ω
    Ω Ω
     Ω
✠ LWHADHL ✠
```

PSALM 4

FOR RESTFUL SLEEP

Recite the psalm three times over a small dish of salt, and invoke the Trinity after each recitation. Sprinkle the salt around the bed.

If evil spirits trouble you in your sleep, place the following symbol above your bed, in conjunction with the blessed salt:

```
          ✠
         A
   ✠  Y     D  ✠
    I will both lay me
    down in peace,
    and sleep: for
    thou, LORD, only
    makest me dwell
   ✠  A  in safety.  O  ✠
         N
          ✠
```

FOR LUCK IN MONEY MATTERS

Write the psalm on a dollar bill, and fold it around a small metal crucifix. Sew this into a piece of green cloth and carry it in your wallet.

PSALM 5

TO OPEN ROADS

On a clean piece of paper, draw the above symbol on one side, and the following planetary square of Mercury on the other:

8	58	59	5	4	62	63	1
49	15	14	52	53	11	10	56
41	23	22	44	45	19	18	48
32	34	35	29	28	38	39	25
40	26	27	37	36	30	31	33
17	47	46	20	21	43	42	24
9	55	54	12	13	51	50	16
64	2	3	61	60	6	7	57

Light 8 grey candles around the talisman and pray the psalm 8 times. Afterwards, roll the talisman towards you and place it in a vial with some quicksilver or gallium, quicksilver being poisonous so be cautious. Seal the vile tight, and sew it into a piece of grey cloth.

To Influence an Authority Figure

Write the name of the person 8 times, and write your name across it 8 times:

JOHN DOE
JOHN DOE
JOHN DOE JOHN DOE JOHN DOE JOHN DOE JOHN DOE JOHN DOE JOHN DOE
JOHN DOE
JOHN DOE

On the back side, inscribe the sigil of Raphael

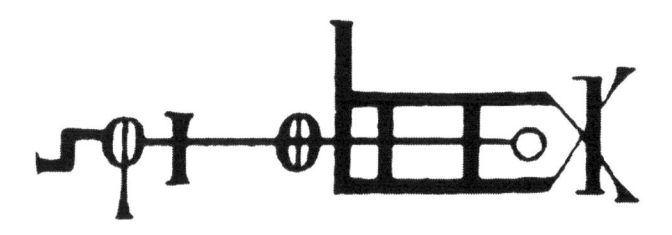

Pray the Psalm 8 times and fumigate the talisman with lavender.

Carry the talisman with you when you go to meet the person.

PSALM 6

FOR EYE TROUBLES

Take two yellow candles and carve the shape of an eye in each one. Set these two candles to light and pray to St. Lucy:

"**Saint Lucy**

Whose beautiful name signifies 'LIGHT'

by the light of faith which God bestowed upon you

increase and preserve His light in my soul

so that I may avoid evil,

Be zealous in the performance of good works

and abhor nothing so much as the blindness and

the darkness of evil and sin.

Obtain for me, by your intercession with God

Perfect vision for my bodily eyes

and the grace to use them for God's greater honour and glory

and the salvation of souls.

St. Lucy, virgin and martyr

hear my prayers and obtain my petitions.

Amen."

Recite the psalm. Repeat this every day for seven days.

TO KNOW WHO YOUR ENEMIES ARE

On the day and hour of Mercury, draw the talisman above on a piece of aluminum. Place it between a yellow and white candle and pray the psalm 8 times. Afterwards, sleep with it under your pillow and your dreams will reveal who your enemies are.

PROTECTION WHILE TRAVELING

```
        P
        A
        T
     ✠  E  ✠
        R
PATERNOSTER
        O
        S
     ✠  T  ✠
        E
        R
```

Write the psalm down on a piece of paper; and the above symbol on the other side. Fold it towards you with some of your hair and nail clippings inside, to make a small packet. Stitch this up in red flannel and wear it near your heart.

PSALM 7

AGAINST WITNESSES IN COURT

Write the names of the witnesses against you on a piece of paper. Over this, copy the psalm and draw a Star of David on top of the whole thing.

Take a piece of beef steak, such as a cut of bottom round, and lay the paper, face down, into the steak. Roll the steak away from you, rolling the paper up with it.

Tie this closed with three pieces of black thread and leave it on a railroad track.

TO INFLUENCE A JUDGE

Begin by lighting a white candle and reciting the following from verse:

Revelations 4:5 - And out of the throne proceeded lightnings and thunderings and voices: and there were seven lamps of fire burning before the throne, which are the seven Spirits of God.

Recite the name of the Judge.

Recite the Psalm.

Repeat with another candle the same set of prayers until you are burning 7 candles, one for each of the seven Spirits of God.

PSALM 8

AN OIL FOR GENERAL BLESSING AND GOOD FORTUNE

Write the psalm on clean paper, and roll it towards you. Place it down into a bottle of olive oil and recite the psalm three times over it, in the name of the Trinity. Use the oil to anoint your doorways, your pocket books, or your self to call upon the grave and power of the Lord.

TO HEAL A SICKLY INFANT

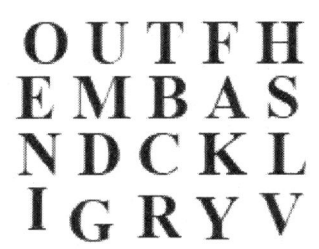

```
O U T F H
E M B A S
N D C K L
I G R Y V
```

On a clean piece of paper, write the magic square above. On the back, write the following signs:

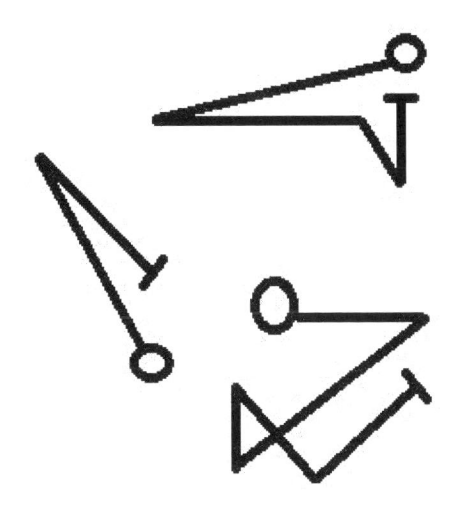

Recite the Psalm 3 times, in honor of the Most Holy Trinity and place the talisman in the baby's pillow or cap.

TO BE HONORED IN ALL THINGS

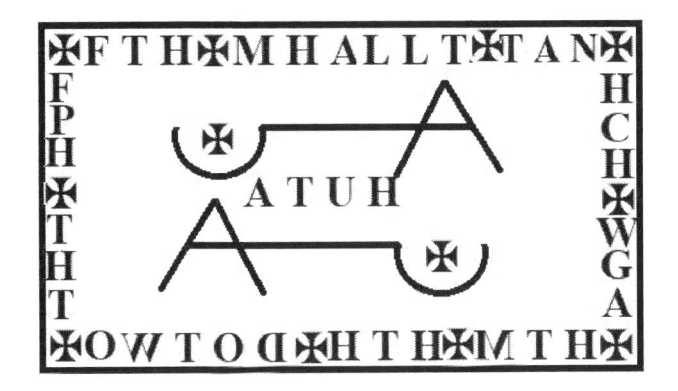

Construct the above seal in the day and hour of Jupiter, the moon increasing. Consecrate it with clove oil and the psalm 4 times.

FOR SUCCESS IN HUNTING OR FISHING

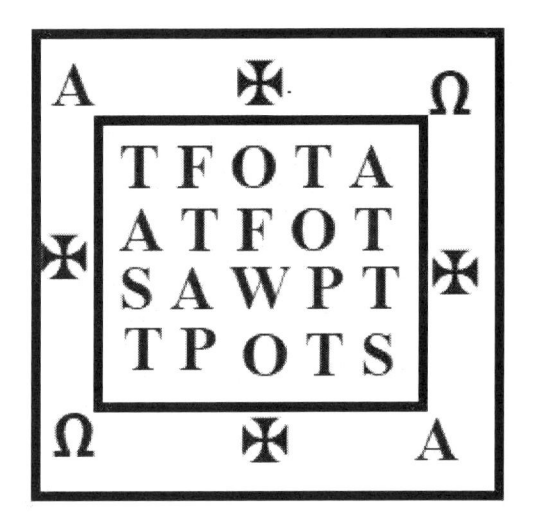

```
A    ✠         Ω
   T F O T A
   A T F O T
✠  S A W P T  ✠
   T P O T S
Ω    ✠         A
```

Make the above seal with blue ink and consecrate it with the psalm three times, in honor of the Trinity. Attach it to your rifle or fishing pole.

PSALM 9

TO REPEL AN ENEMY

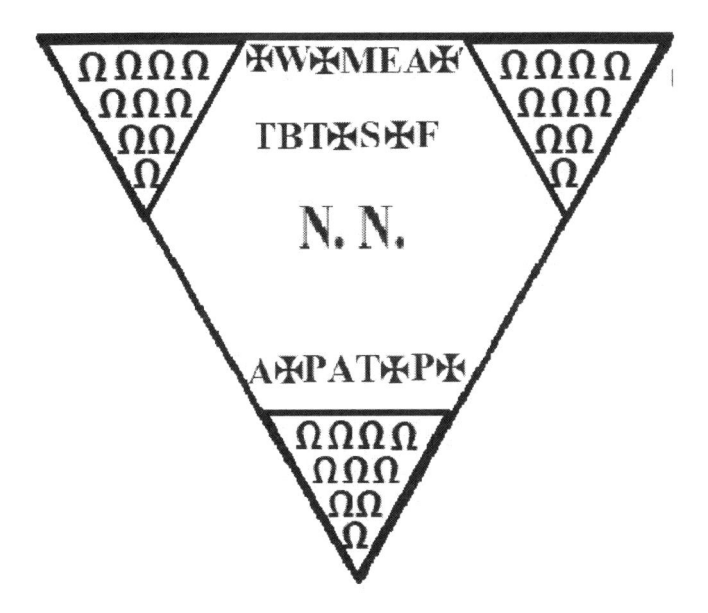

```
   ΩΩΩΩ  ✠W✠MEA✠  ΩΩΩΩ
    ΩΩΩ              ΩΩΩ
     ΩΩ   TBT✠S✠F    ΩΩ
      Ω                Ω

              N. N.


          A✠PAT✠P✠

           ΩΩΩΩ
            ΩΩΩ
             ΩΩ
              Ω
```

Make 20 copies of the seal, and where the seal shows **N.N.** write the name of your enemy.

On a Saturday during the waning moon, make a circle of 9 candles and stand within it. Recite the psalm, one verse at a time. After each verse, set one of the seals on fire with the flame of the black candle in the western most direction, and drop it in a metal dish.

After you have burned every paper, pray to the Lord over the smoldering ashes of the seals to repel your enemy.

Take the ashes and any leftover candle wax and either bury it in a cemetery, or throw it over your left shoulder into a river.

TO FREE A PRISONER

> EL✠ADONAI✠TOT✠R✠F✠AW BA✠TO ARI
> Lord, my redeemer; free me ✠✠✠

Have the prisoner carry the piece of paper; or should that be impossible, to write the seal directly on his skin and daily pray the psalm three times in honor of the Most Holy Trinity.

TO CATCH A MURDERER

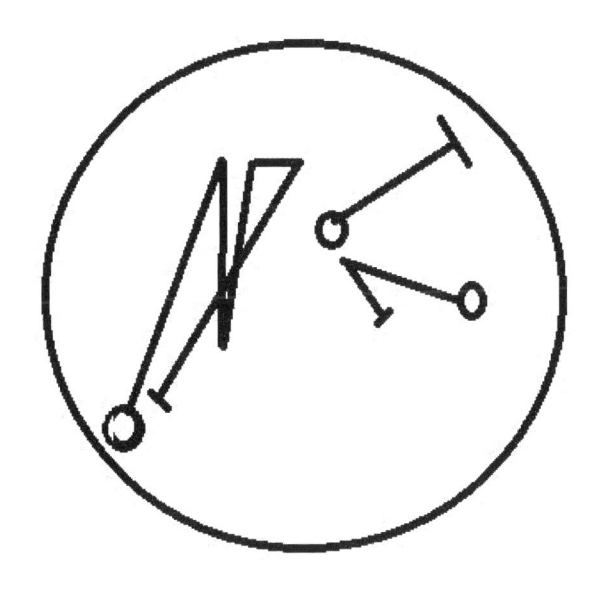

On a piece of iron or steel, draw the above signs; and on the other side, the following magical square:

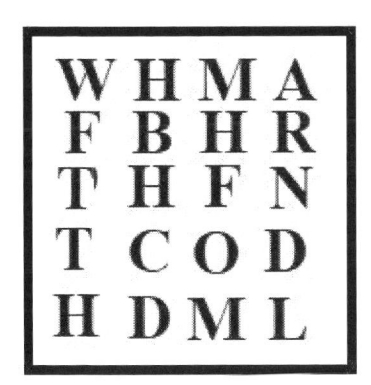

W	H	M	A
F	B	H	R
T	H	F	N
T	C	O	D
H	D	M	L

Recite the psalm 9 times over the iron; and in between each recitation; recite **"Lord, reveal the sinner and his works."**

Afterwards, dispose of this in the grave of the victim; or at a courthouse.

RETURN TO SENDER

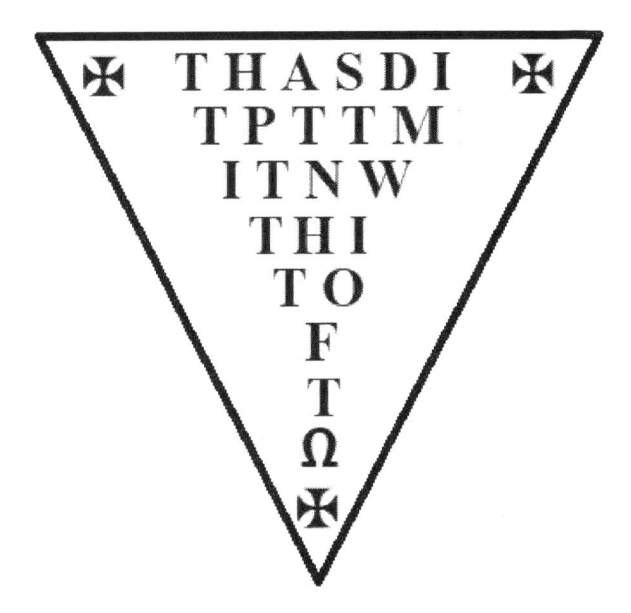

```
✠ T H A S D I ✠
  T P T T M
  I T N W
  T H I
  T O
  F
  T
  Ω
  ✠
```

Scratch the above seal onto a rusty piece of metal. Boil this seal with your own urine while reciting the psalm 9 times. Afterwards, take the urine and seal and pour it down a drain away from your home.

PSALM 10

DEFENSE AGAINST EVIL SPIRITS

Bless some white chalk with holy water, and mark the following seal under your doormat, bed, area rug, etc. Sprinkle it with holy water and recite the psalm three times in honor of the Most Holy Trinity.

THAT THE TRUTH ABOUT A PERSON WILL BE KNOWN

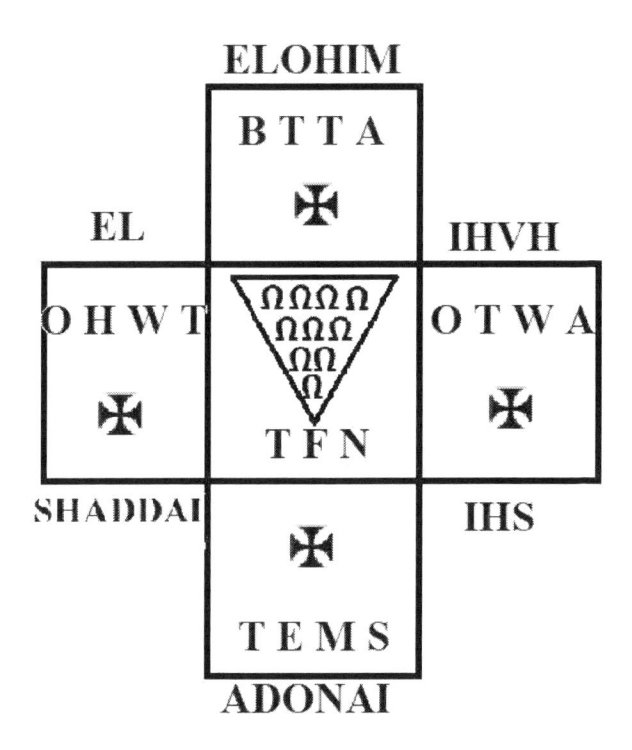

                    ELOHIM

            ┌─────────────────┐
            │   BTTA   │
            │   ✠   │
    ┌───────┼─────────────────┼───────┐
EL │ OHWT │   ΩΩΩΩ /   │ OTWA │ **IHVH**
        │   │   ΩΩΩ /   │   │
        │   │   ΩΩ /   │   │
        │   ✠   │   Ω▽   │   ✠   │
        │   │   TFN   │   │
    └───────┼─────────────────┼───────┘
SHADDAI │   ✠   │ **IHS**
            │   │
            │   TEMS   │
            └─────────────────┘
                  ADONAI

Draw the seal on a white plate in black in, and on the back write the person's name.

For 9 nights, light a black candle in the center of the plate and pray the psalm. Afterwards, speak the person's full name to the four cardinal directions.

After this is complete, break the dish in the person's yard.

PSALM 11

PROTECTION FROM THE WORK OF YOUR ENEMIES

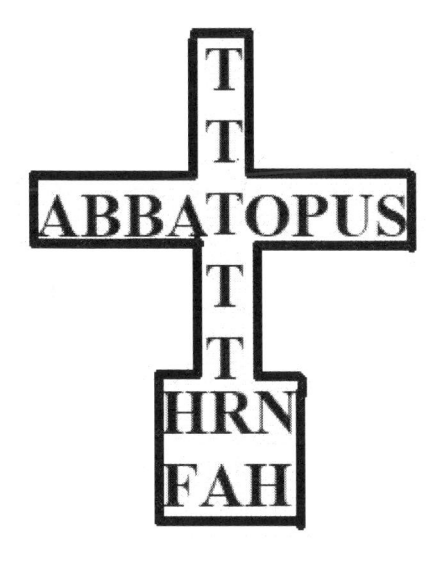

```
      T
      T
ABBATOPUS
      T
      T
     HRN
     FAH
```

Pray the psalm 9 times over a bowl of rainwater in which you have a mirror soaking. Afterwards, take the mirror out and allow it to air dry.

The seal is to be painted with black ink on the surface of a mirror and hung over your doorway, mirror facing outwards.

PROTECT FROM WITCHCRAFT

The above same seal can also be written upon a piece of silver and carried as a ward against witchcraft.

PSALM 12

TO SILENCE A LIAR AND GOSSIP

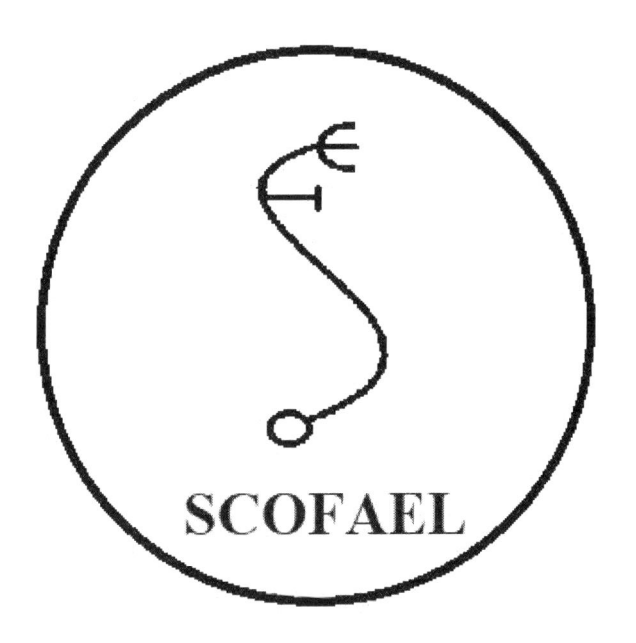

SCOFAEL

Write the seal on a clean piece of paper; and on the back side write "ADONAY + N.N.+ ADONAY"

Burn a black candle on top of the seal while praying the psalm 9 times. In between each recitation; say "Scofael, Adonay, cut off the flattering lips of N.N."

Afterwards, hide the seal in your bible.

TO PROTECT YOUR CHILDREN FROM GOING DOWN THE WRONG PATH

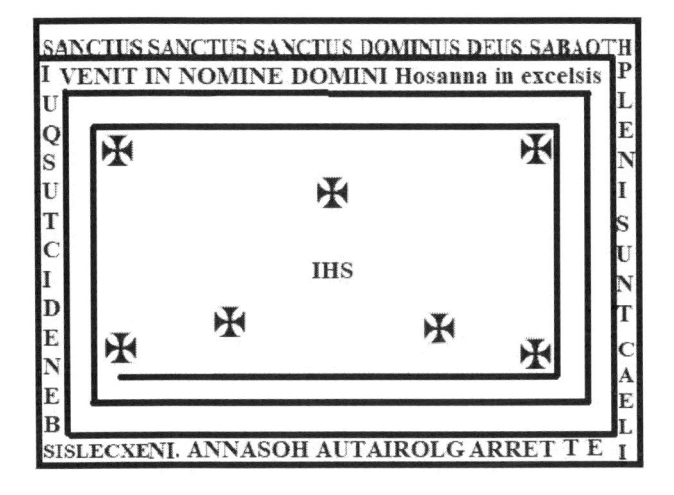

```
SANCTUS SANCTUS SANCTUS DOMINUS DEUS SABAOTH
  VENIT IN NOMINE DOMINI Hosanna in excelsis
           ✠                    ✠
                    ✠
                   IHS
              ✠         ✠
           ✠                    ✠
SISLECXENI. ANNASOH AUTAIROLG ARRET T E
```

Paint or embroider the above seal on a piece of white cloth. Pray the psalm three times over the cloth and in the center place a lock of your child's hair, wrapped in a piece of wool. Fold the cloth up and place it inside of a bible. Tie the bible closed crossways with red cord and keep it in a cedar box in a safe place.

FOR ASSISTANCE IN A CIVIL SUIT

> For the oppression of the poor, for the sighing of the needy, now will I arise, saith the Lord; I will set him in safety from him that puffeth at him.
>
> ✠ ✠ ✠

Write the above verses and crosses on a piece of clean paper; and on the back, write the name of the judge.

Light a red candle, white candle, and gold candle in a triangle around the seal and pray the psalm seven times. Afterwards, roll the paper towards you; verse side outwards, and carry it in your left pocket to court.

PSALM 13

FOR THE SICK

```
┌──────────────────────────────────────────┐
│                   ✠                      │
│                  N.N.                    │
│                                          │
│  YHATRU ✠ YNTHI ✠ MERMIH ✠ SREYNT ✠ SAL  │
│                                          │
│        Lord Jesus, Physician of my soul. │
└──────────────────────────────────────────┘
```

Copy the seal and write the sick person's name where the N.N. is shown. Have three believers pray the psalm for the benefit of the person over the seal.

If the person is not to know about the seal, hide it in the spine of a bible and place it in the room with them. If they are an unbeliever; or for some reason a bible would not be appropriate; hide the seal under their mattress.

TO PROTECT YOUR BUSINESS

```
┌──────────────────────────────────────────────────┐
│ Y.VV.Y.L.S.Y.N.G.V.N. ✠ ADONAY ✠ BEHEHATH DEA ✠ L.T.B.O.V.N.T. │
│                       N.N.                       │
└──────────────────────────────────────────────────┘
```

Write the above across a dollar pill, with your initials in place of the N.N. and place it over the door of your place of business. Every day before business, take the dollar bill and recite the psalm over it, while facing east.

PSALM 14

TO PUNISH A CHEATING SPOUSE

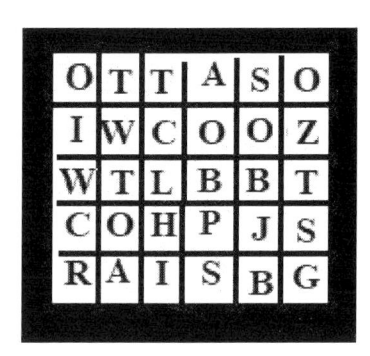

O	T	T	A	S	O
I	W	C	O	O	Z
W	T	L	B	B	T
C	O	H	P	J	S
R	A	I	S	B	G

Make the above seal on lead and tie one of their dirty socks or underwear around it. Deposit this into the grave of a married couple and pray the psalm towards the West, while thinking of the pain your cheating spouse has caused you.

TO PUNISH A WRONGDOER

1. The Psalm can be copied and burned to ashes and introduced into the person's food.
2. The Psalm can be spoken three times over the person's shirt or garment.
3. The Psalm can be recited over vinegar and pour on their doorstep.

4. The Psalm can be recited three times over water collected during a lightning storm. This can be introduced to their food, coffee, sprinkled on their shoes or clothing; added to their bottle of shampoo - anything.

PSALM 15

ASSISTANCE IN GETTING A LOAN

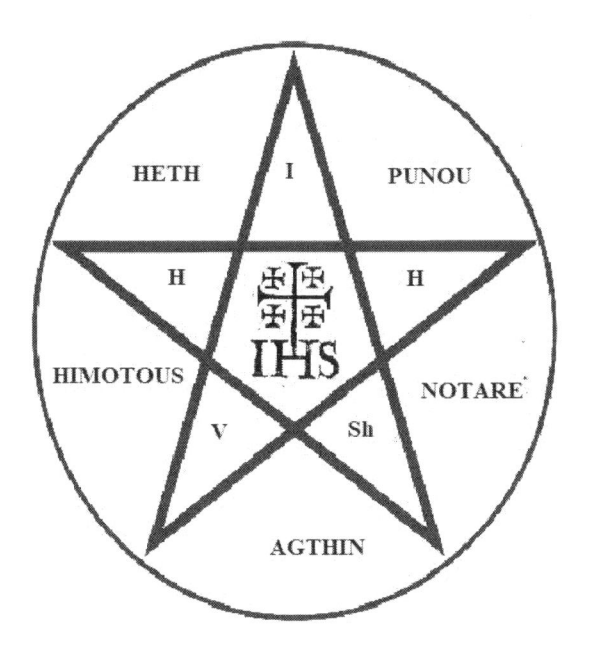

(Seal: pentagram within a circle, with labels HETH, I, PUNOU, H, H, HIMOTOUS, NOTARE, V, Sh, AGTHIN, and central IHS with cross.)

Draw the above seal in gold ink and when the Sun first rises above the horizon on a Wednesday, recite the psalm 8 times, while holding the seal towards the sun. Carry it with you in your wallet.

TO KEEP A PERSON QUIET

H	A	N
H	D	N
U	A	I

HETH ABAC NOVITH HISTOR DETH NENOTAK UPARE AGAH ISNE

Write the above square on two pieces of wood. Take a photo of the person you wish to keep quiet, and use a needle and thread to stitch the mouth of the photo closed and chant the above incantation nine times over the photo. Take the two magic squares and sandwich the photo in between them. Bind the pieces of wood together and place them under a heavy rock and recite the psalm three times, facing the North.

TO KEEP YOUR PARTNER FAITHFUL

HETH ✠ VAV ✠ PAV ✠
N.N.
✠ RAST ✠ TRU ✠ INHI ✠ HE

Write the above seal on dough and bake it into bread, pie, or some food. Where N.N. is indicated, write your initials. While it is cooking pray the psalm seven times.

The same seal is written on a piece of paper in your own blood; but this time the N.N. is to be the initials of your partner. Wrap some of your partner's hair in this seal and sew it up into a piece of red cloth. Keep this hidden from him and pray the psalm over it once a week.

PSALM 16

TO MAKE YOUR FORMER PARTNER SORROWFUL FOR HAVING LEFT YOU

T	B	T
T	O	V
N	N	L

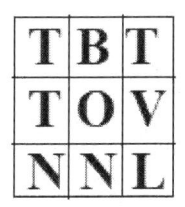

Draw the above magic square over the face of a photograph of the former partner in your own blood. Pray the psalm over the photo and then pray the following seven times; after each recitation, say the person's entire name:

THESHA BEM THASANG THERDO OB VIL NONTUTH NIM LI

TO REVERSE CROSSED CONDITIONS

```
    FOTHOUN
     LEMYS
     IHNEV
      TUSUT
      HOTO
       SEC
        ✠
        ✠
```

Draw the above psalm on a clean piece of paper and hold it in your left hand every day at dawn, bowing on your right knee. Recite the psalm. At sundown, bow on your left knee while holding the paper in your right hand and recite the psalm. Do this for nine days in a row and wear the seal around your neck.

TO OVERCOME OBSTACLES

IHS ADONAY EL BEM BEHIS AMYR HIS NOBEM

Carry the above names tied to your left wrist and recite the psalm before going toward your work.

TO PROTECT YOUR HOME

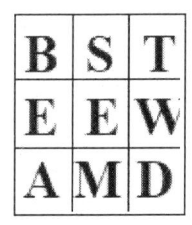

B	S	T
E	E	W
A	M	D

Make the above square on four pieces of metal and fumigate them with myrrh while praying the psalm four times. Bury the four squares at the four corners of the home.

Should you live in an apartment; attack them to the four walls; or the four walls of your room.

TO EXCELL IN YOUR WORK

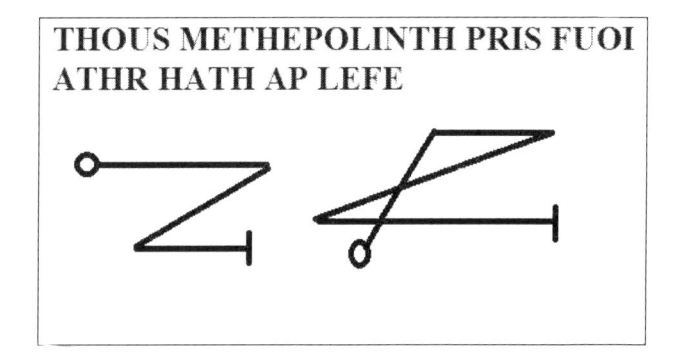

THOUS METHEPOLINTH PRIS FUOI ATHR HATH AP LEFE

Make the above seal and consecrate it with the psalm. Roll this seal towards you and carry it in a small vial of olive oil in which a piece of cedar wood has been placed.

PSALM 17

FOR SAFETY WHILE TRAVELING

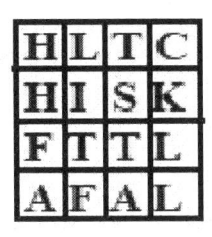

H	L	T	C
H	I	S	K
F	T	T	L
A	F	A	L

Make the above square on aluminum on a Wednesday during the hour of Mercury. Pray the psalm 8 times and fumigate it with lavender.

FOR INVISIBILITY

HIMUT SOTWI
HIMUT SOTWI
HIMUT SOTWI

The above seal, on aluminum or clean paper, fashioned on the day and hour of Mercury. Fumigate with fern seed while reciting the psalm 8 times.

PSALM 18

THE CROSS OF ST. LAZARUS OF JERUSALEM

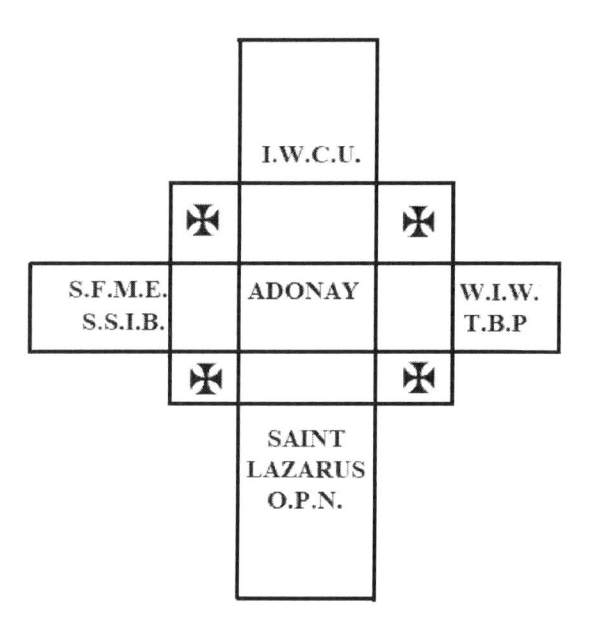

		I.W.C.U.		
	✠		✠	
S.F.M.E. S.S.I.B.		ADONAY		W.I.W. T.B.P
	✠		✠	
		SAINT LAZARUS O.P.N.		

To be used in conjunction with the psalm for healing and protection.

TO SEND SOMEONE'S EVIL BACK TO THEM

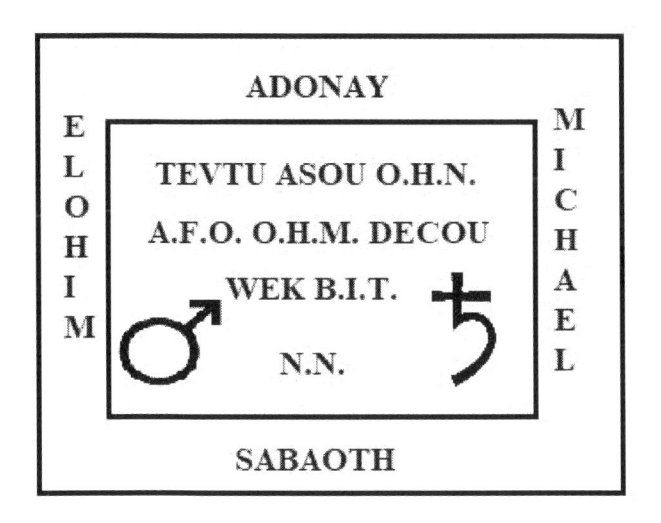

```
           ADONAY
    ┌─────────────────────┐
  E │                     │ M
  L │  TEVTU ASOU O.H.N.  │ I
  O │                     │ C
  H │  A.F.O. O.H.M. DECOU│ H
  I │     WEK B.I.T.   ♄  │ A
  M │  ♂     N.N.         │ E
    │                     │ L
    └─────────────────────┘
           SABAOTH
```

Mark the above seal on a piece of clean paper in walnut gall ink. Replace N.N. with the person's name.

Place this seal in an oil lamp with five iron nails. Light the oil lamp at a crossroads, and recite the psalm. Leave the lamp burning and do not look back.

TO DESTROY YOUR OPPOSITION

```
      I
      H
      P
 ✠    M      ✠
     ┌─┐
 ATTW│C│NDTA
     └─┘
      E
 ✠    A      ✠
      O
      T
```

Carry the above seal in red ink wrapped around an iron nail and consecrated with the psalm five times.

TO CONTROL AND DOMINATE OTHERS

```
ASATH✠OMET✠SOMET✠STRAS✠SUTUM
ASATH✠OMET✠SOMET✠STRAS✠SUTUM
ASATH✠OMET✠SOMET✠STRAS✠SUTUM
```

Write the seal on clean paper in your own blood and consecrate it with the psalm five times and fumigate it with peppercorns.

THE THIEF'S CROSS

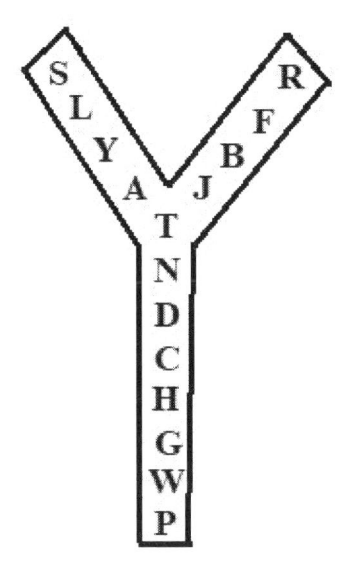

Mark the above letters on a forked stick and recite the psalm three times over it in honor of the Most Holy Trinity. Anoint it with olive oil and plant it before your door.

Should you know a person has stolen from you, wrap their name around the thieve's cross and bury it upside down in a bottle of vinegar.

PSALM 19

FOR DIFFICULTY CONCEIVING AND GENERAL PREGNANCY PROTECTION

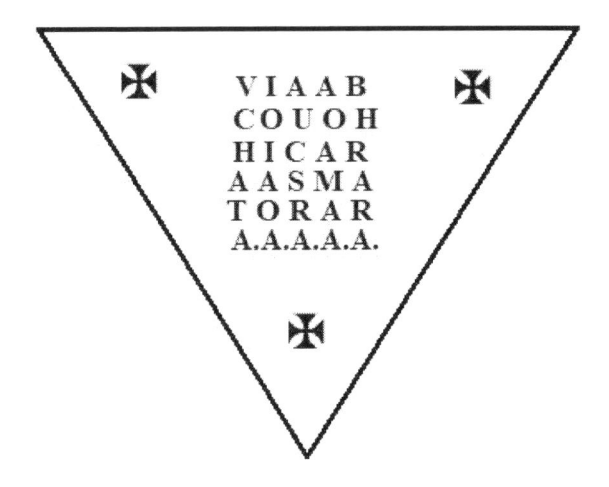

```
✠        VIAAB        ✠
         COUOH
         HICAR
         AASMA
         TORAR
        A.A.A.A.A.
            ✠
```

Mark the above seal on seven bay leaves and fumigate the room with them.

Should this be unfeasible; mark the seal on the seven leaves and lay them under the middle of the mattress.

For Assistance in Court

Write the names of the judge, prosecutor, and witnesses against you on a piece of paper.

Over this, write the following names:

THELO ADONAY IPECO TESOTHE TOT ADONAY ISE

Pray the psalm while facing the south four times and recite the names above four times while holding the piece of paper in your left hand. Afterwards, place it in your shoe.

TO BE WARNED OF DANGERS

```
MOREB TITH SERVA
MOREB TITH SERV
MOREB TITH SER
MOREB TITH SE
MOREB TITH S
MOREB TITH
MOREB TIT
MOREB TI
MOREB T
MOREB
MORE
MOR
Mo
M
```

Place the seal under your pillow and every night before bed pray the Psalm and the Lord's prayer three times and ask the Lord to reveal any dangers to you in your dreams.

To Make Someone Contact You

```
TIN SPENOR LAVET VIS NOHEA
N.N.
TIN SPENOR LAVET VIS NOHEA
N.N.
TIN SPENOR LAVET VIS NOHEA
```

Write the above psalm eight times on eight different pieces of paper. On the first N.N. write your name; and on the second, the name of the person you wish to contact you.

Recite the psalm and burn one seal. Do this eight times outside, so the smoke can freely arise into the air and see the person out.

PSALM 20

TO GET A DEBT REPAID

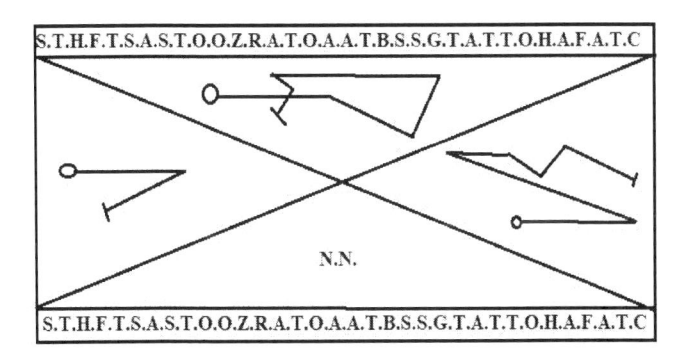

```
S.T.H.F.T.S.A.S.T.O.O.Z.R.A.T.O.A.A.T.B.S.S.G.T.A.T.T.O.H.A.F.A.T.C
                           N.N.
S.T.H.F.T.S.A.S.T.O.O.Z.R.A.T.O.A.A.T.B.S.S.G.T.A.T.T.O.H.A.F.A.T.C
```

Write the above seal on clean paper and the person's name where N.N. is designated. Consecrate it with holy water and the psalm, plus 23 Glorias.

Fold the paper towards you and nail it above your door.

TO PROTECT A CAR FROM ACCIDENTS

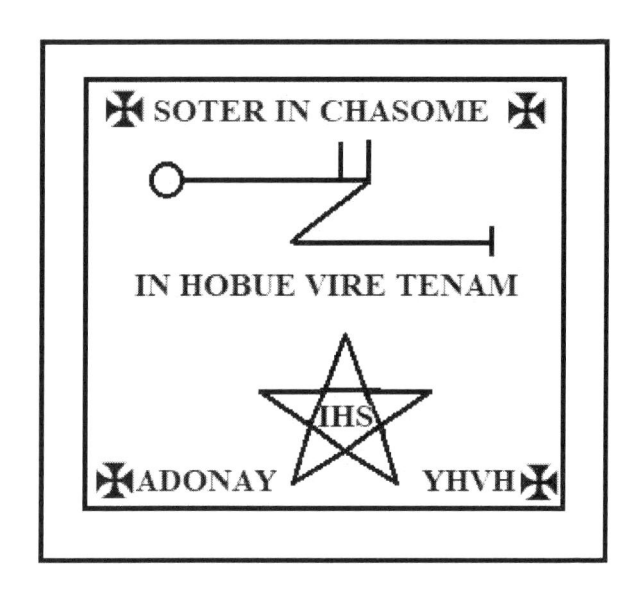

```
┌─────────────────────────────────┐
│    ✠ SOTER IN CHASOME ✠         │
│                                 │
│         [sigil]                 │
│                                 │
│      IN HOBUE VIRE TENAM        │
│                                 │
│          [pentagram with IHS]   │
│   ✠ADONAY            YHVH✠      │
└─────────────────────────────────┘
```

Make the above seal on metal and wash it in river water seven times after reciting the psalm over it. Keep it in the vehicle you wish to be protected.

TO OVERCOME YOUR COMPETITION

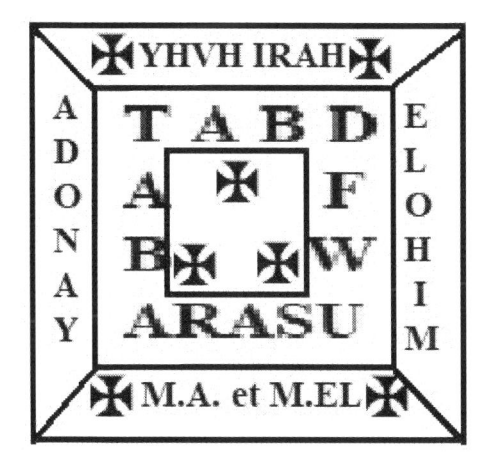

Draw this seal on a clean plate with pomegranate juice and pray the psalm seven times over it. Wash the seal off with water into a bowl and drink the water.

PSALM 21

TO CALM A STORM

```
  \T.S.T.M.T.T.T./
   \B.W.T.S.M.R/
    \T.A.V.T.S/
     \A.T.F.O/
        T
```

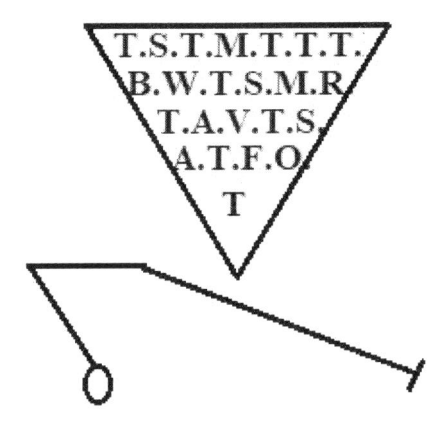

Make the above triangle on tin; and the seal on the back. Fumigate it nine times with cedar while reciting the psalm. When a storm comes, take the seal out and use it to mark the sign of the cross across the sky while praying the psalm.

TO PROTECT A BOAT

✠
A
D
O
N
✠SAIOAIT✠
N
A
✠THEKITYSAHOV✠
G
E
S
H
E
R
E
✠

Make the above seal on a piece of ash in the blood of a red rooster. Pray the psalm over it seven times and tie it onto the boat.

TO BE HONORED IN ALL THINGS

20	8	15	21	19	5
20	20	5	19	20	1
3	18	15	23	14	15
6	16	21	18	5	7
15	12	4	15	14	8
9	19	8	5	1	4

Make the above square on silver when the moon is full and well aspected and fumigate it 9 times with camphor; reciting the psalm once for each fumigation.

TO BE TRUSTED BY ALL

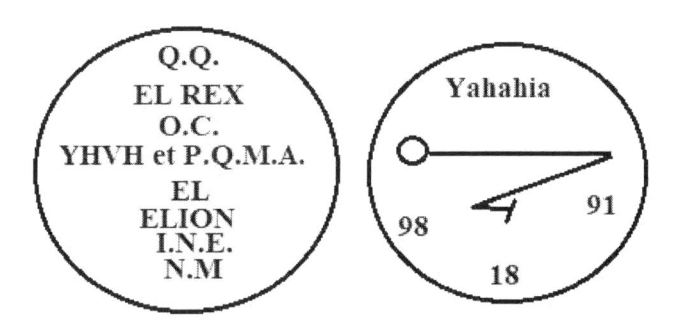

Q.Q.
EL REX
O.C.
YHVH et P.Q.M.A.
EL
ELION
I.N.E.
N.M

Yahahia
98
91
18

Make the above seal in silver with the moon well aspected. Fumigate with camphor 9 times, reciting the psalm once for each fumigation.

PSALM 22

PROTECTION FROM WEAPONS AND ANIMALS

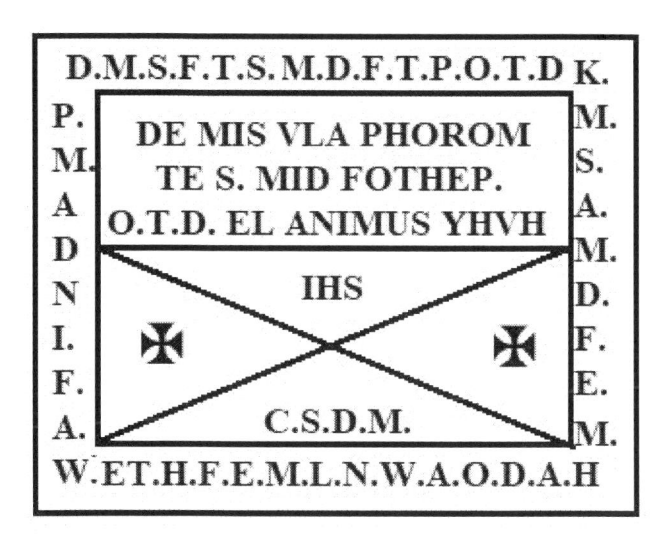

```
D.M.S.F.T.S. M.D.F.T.P.O.T.D K.
P.  ┌─────────────────────────┐ M.
M.  │  DE MIS VLA PHOROM      │ S.
A   │   TE S. MID FOTHEP.     │ A.
D   │  O.T.D. EL ANIMUS YHVH  │ M.
N   │         IHS             │ D.
I.  │    ✠            ✠       │ F.
F.  │                         │ E.
A.  │        C.S.D.M.         │ M.
    └─────────────────────────┘
W.ET.H.F.E.M.L.N.W.A.O.D.A.H
```

Construct the above seal in lead, Saturn well aspected for the procedure; fumigate with myrrh three times with the psalm recited three times.

TO PUT YOUR CHILDREN BACK ON THE RIGHT PATH

9	23	3	22
20	6	20	23
20	1	13	7
6	13	9	2

A small wooden box is obtained or made, and the above magic square made on the outside top of the lid, as well as the inside of the lid. The bottom of the box will also have the square. Around the inside and outside sides of the box, mark the words:

IVA CAV TEFOT TEV TAM EL F.M.M.B.

Inside the box, wrapped in red cloth, place a lock of hair, photo, or some object belonging to the child. Every day pray the psalm three times in honor of the Holy Trinity along with the Lord's Prayer for the welfare of your child's life and the conversion of bad habits.

PSALM 23

TO DREAM THE ANSWER

```
ADONAY I.M.S. ISANOV ✠ ✠ ✠ STIVAT
I.E.A.T.T.E.O.O.I.N.V.R.T.T.P.A.T.B.M.I.T
.P.O.M.E.T.A.M.O.R.I.M.C.R.O.S.G.E.T.M.
HE REM SOHELETH MEI TEPAT SOPH
A.I.M.S.I.H.M.L.G.H.M.E.S.H.R.S.M.T.S.R.
I.E.A. TIVA TOUT EVA OTES OD IVIVEA
☿ S.F.M.A.T.D.O.M.L.A.I.W.D.I.B.A.F.E ☽
   NEVOTA VIMET RATIS TECOME.
HEM MET LEDIN GEPA HEL MEB ET
RIEOU ESVO TETRAGRAMMATON
         E. TETRAGRAMMATON
```

Make the above seal on clean paper in purple ink; and pray the psalm over it three times before bed. Place it under your pillow.

FOR FINANCIAL NEEDS

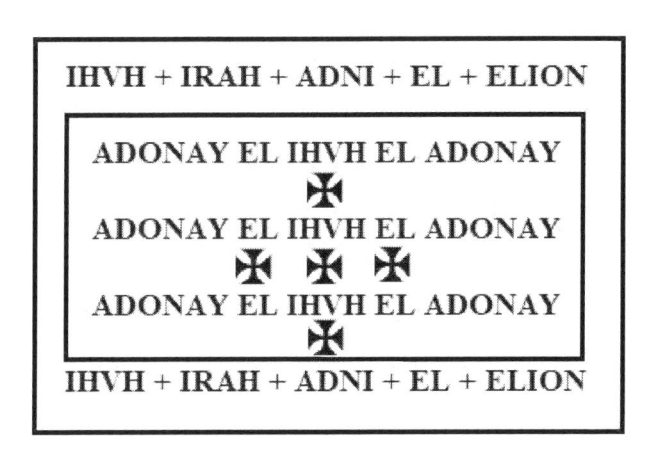

```
IHVH + IRAH + ADNI + EL + ELION
   ADONAY EL IHVH EL ADONAY
              ✠
   ADONAY EL IHVH EL ADONAY
         ✠   ✠   ✠
   ADONAY EL IHVH EL ADONAY
              ✠
IHVH + IRAH + ADNI + EL + ELION
```

Burn a green candle on the seal and pray the psalm. Do this for three days in a row. Carry the seal in your wallet or purse.

PSALM 24

FOR ASSISTANCE FINDING A HOME

```
┌─────────────────────────────┐
│   ADONAI HA'ARETZ           │
│                             │
│  et T.T.D.T     et F.T.     │
│                             │
│       MALKUTH               │
└─────────────────────────────┘
```

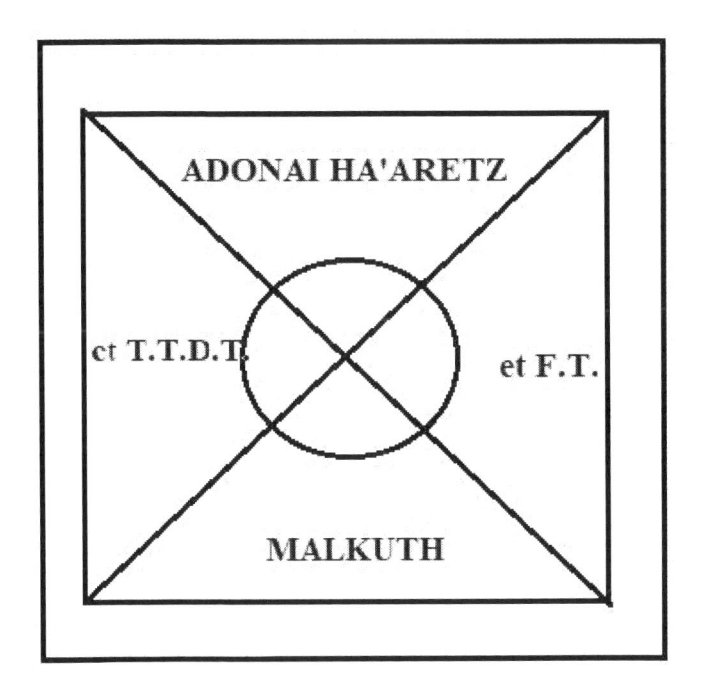

Carry the above seal with a lodestone and three iron nails in a red bag. Recite the psalm three times over it.

TO REVEAL THE THIEF

F	V	Y
H	T	C
L	N	S
P	R	W

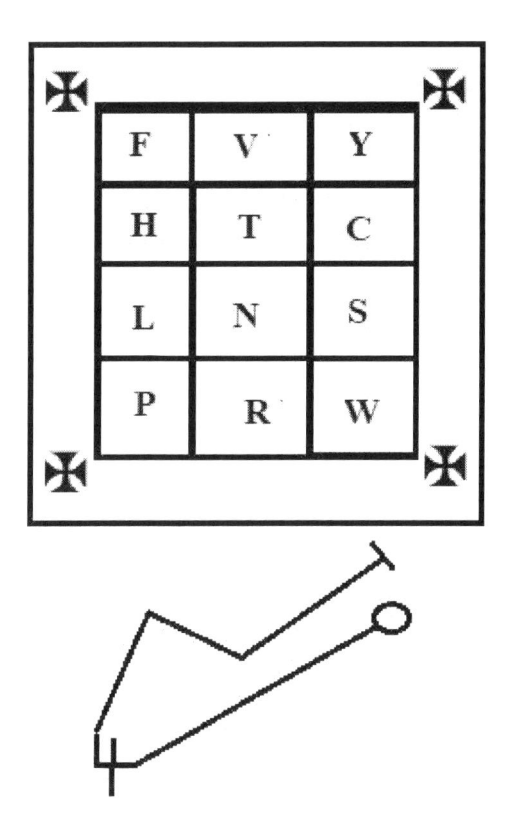

Place the square, with the symbol below on the back, under your pillow and pray the psalm three times before going to sleep.

FOR ADDICTIONS

H	S	R	T
B	F	L	A
A	R	F	T
Y	O	H	S

Draw this seal in myrrh ink on a piece of white cloth. Wrap a photo or belonging of the addict in the cloth and pray the psalm over it three times every day at sunset, facing the west.

TO OPEN DOORS FOR OPPORTUNITY

L	V	I	H	O
I	G	A	B	I
L	V	I	E	D
A	T	K	O	G
S	C	I	I	A

Carry the seal, written in red ink and consecrated with the psalm three times.

PSALM 25

TO OVERCOME SHAME

I	T	I	T
L	M	N	B
A	L	N	M
E	T	O	M

Should you wish a shameful moment to be forgotten or overlooked, make the above square on a piece of aluminum during the new moon and recite the psalm eight times over it.

TO NOT GET LOST

W	P	M
T	A	T
S	T	M

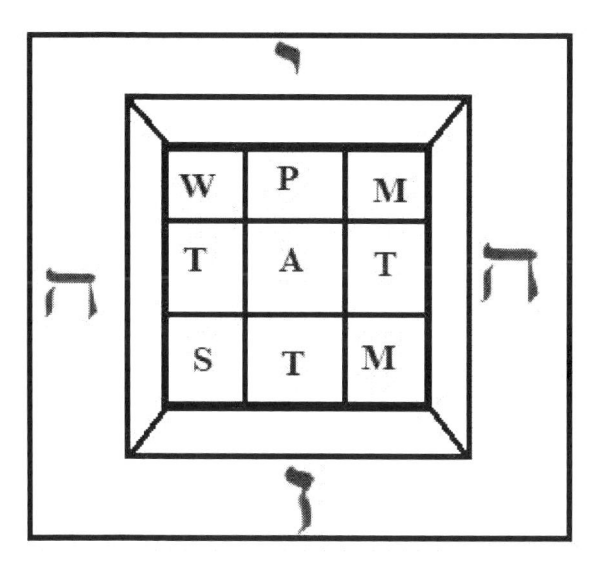

Mark the above seal in blue ink and pray the psalm over it eight times. Fumigate it with lavender.

TO PREVENT ARREST OR CAPTURE

M	E	A	E
T	A	F	H
S	P	M	F
O	O	T	N

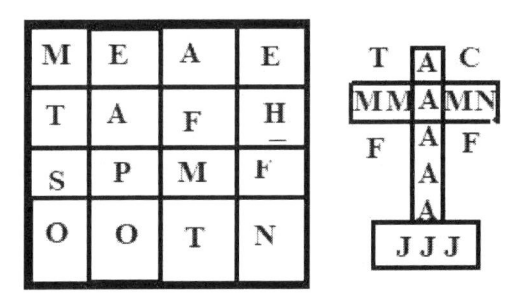

```
    T A C
    M M A M N
    F A F
      A
      A
      A
    J J J
```

Make the above square on a clean piece of paper; and the word-cross on the back. Consecrate this seal by fumigating with lavender and fern seed; and reciting the psalm 8 times.

Carry the seal in a piece of grey cloth around the neck.

PSALM 26

TO AVOID BLAME

V	I	M	E	A
D	O	N	A	I
F	I	H	L	A
B	A	M	E	L

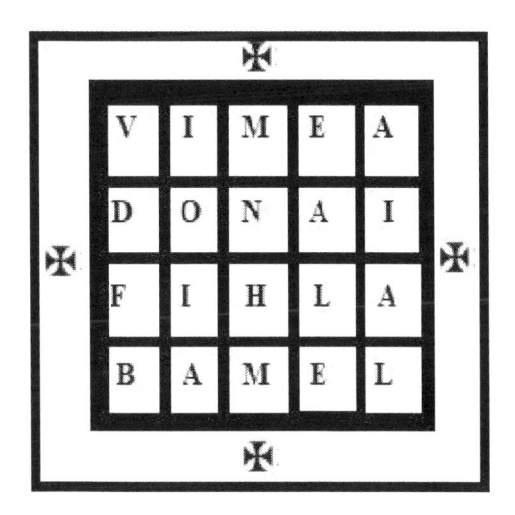

Make the above square on sheepskin parchment or clean paper with your own blood mixed with a bit of powdered myrrh.

Wear it around your neck, suspended in a small vial of blessed olive oil.

TO DRIVE AWAY DECEITFUL PEOPLE

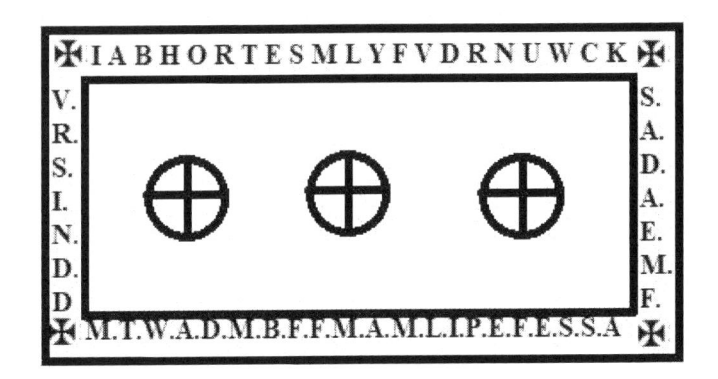

```
✠ I A B H O R T E S M L Y F V D R N U W C K ✠
V.                                              S.
R.                                              A.
S.                                              D.
I.      ⊕        ⊕        ⊕                     A.
N.                                               E.
D.                                               M.
D.                                               F.
✠ M.T.W.A.D.M.B.F.F.M.A.M.L.I.P.E.F.E.S.S.A ✠
```

This seal can be used in various ways. It can be carried on the person, placed above the door; or if you wish to test a person, place it under a chair they have to sit in. If they become uncomfortable or leave quickly, you know they harbor ill towards you.

Make the seal on clean paper and consecrated it by praying the psalm over it three times for your intention.

ASSISTANCE IN LIFE

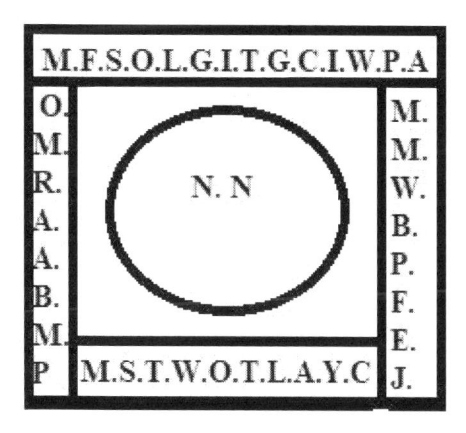

```
┌─────────────────────────────────┐
│  M.F.S.O.L.G.I.T.G.C.I.W.P.A    │
│ O.┌─────────────────────┐ M.    │
│ M.│                     │ M.    │
│ R.│        N. N         │ W.    │
│ A.│                     │ B.    │
│ A.│                     │ P.    │
│ B.│                     │ F.    │
│ M.└─────────────────────┘ E.    │
│ P   M.S.T.W.O.T.L.A.Y.C   J.    │
└─────────────────────────────────┘
```

Should you be troubled by constant setbacks and difficulties, carry the above seal over your heart, consecrated with the psalm 7 times. When you go to pray to the Lord for assistance, hold the seal in your right hand.

PSALM 27

PROTECTION AND REVERSAL

```
        JAH I.M. LUX ET M. S.
    W ┌─────────────────────┐ O
    S │                     │ M
    I │         O           │ L
    F │          \          │ O
    A │           N         │ W
    S │          / \        │ S
    T │         /   \       │ I
    S │        ⊥            │ B
      └─────────────────────┘ A
        W.T.W.A.A.M.T.D.M
        I.I.M.E.A.M.F.W.W.S.A.F
```

Mark the above seal, and for 7 days light a white candle on it and pray the Psalm 7 times with devotion. The seal may then be carried, placed above the bed or door, or incorporated into charms.

PROTECTION FROM SLANDER

```
DON✠TUMEO TOT DEO✠EFO FAVI RUPA
         ✠MES MALIACCU✠
           FIAT FIAT FIAT
               I.N.R.I
```

If you know the name of the slanderers, write them on the back of the seal in black ink, and keep it in an earthenware jar of dirt from a cemetery with iron filings.

If you do not, make the seal when the moon is new, and sew it up in red cloth with salt. Consecrate the seal by praying the psalm four times over it, presenting the seal to the four corners of the earth as you do so.

PSALM 28

TO PUNISH AN EVIL DOER

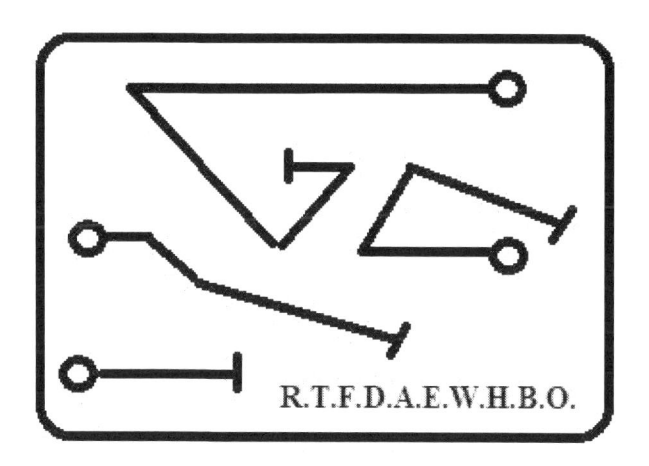

R.T.F.D.A.E.W.H.B.O.

Make the above seal on a sheet of lead on a Saturday during the hour of Saturn. On the back, write the name of the enemy. Take the seal to a cemetery and drive a nail through it onto the west side of a tree. Recite the psalm 9 times, then turn around and leave without looking back.

PROTECTION FROM WITCHCRAFT

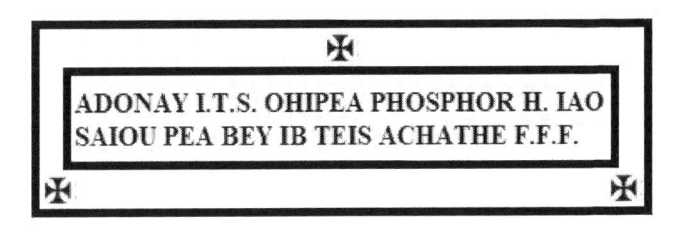

> ✠
> ADONAY I.T.S. OHIPEA PHOSPHOR H. IAO
> SAIOU PEA BEY IB TEIS ACHATHE F.F.F.
> ✠   ✠

Write the seal above on blessed palm with red ink. Pray the psalm three times over it, and burn it to ashes. Mix the ashes with holy water, and drink the water three times, in the name of the Most Holy Trinity.

PSALM 29

FOR RAIN

Mark the above seal in silver and consecrate it with the psalm. Set this is an open vessel outside under the sky.

TO GIVE STRENGTH TO YOUR VOICE

Should you be in a position regarding public speaking, court, or in any position where your voice must be heard; mark the above psalm on your throat with ink made from blessed palm ash mixed with water from a thunderstorm. Draw it over your throat while facing the sunrise, and recite the psalm three times, in honor of the Most Holy Trinity. It may then be washed off.

To Hold Influence Over Others

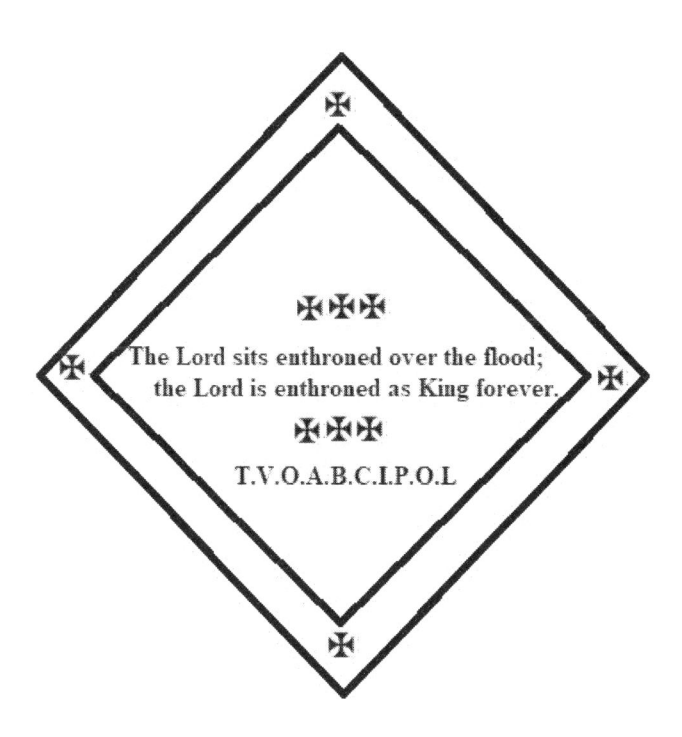

✠
The Lord sits enthroned over the flood;
the Lord is enthroned as King forever.
✠✠✠
T.V.O.A.B.C.I.P.O.L

The above seal should me fashioned and taken to nine Sunday masses. When the priest gives the benediction, hold the seal to receive it. After each mass, pray the Psalm over the seal.

The Psalm is then work around the neck as an amulet.

TO SEE THE GLORY OF THE LORD

THEVO OTEL TITOA ASTRI
✠
THEBA ANHI TELELA
✠
ALC GLORIA
✠
I.H.S.

PSALM 30

To Rise Above Your Foes

I	V	E	X	V
A	D	O	N	A
H	F	I	L	I
M	E	O	V	O
T	E	D	E	A
D	N	O	L	E
M	E	G	O	M

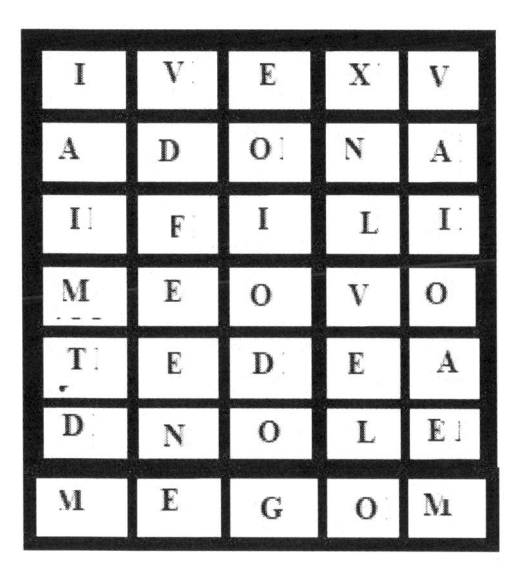

Construct the seal by reciting the psalm each time you write one of the letters, so as to imbue each letter with the full essence of the Psalm. Place this seal above your bed, and say the Lord's Prayer three times before you sleep each night.

FOR HEALING

```
        ✠
       /\
      /  \
     /    \
    / I.C.T.Y.F.H.A.Y.H.M. \
   /  ┌─────────────┐  \
  /   │  YHVH ADONAI │   \
 /    └─────────────┘    \
/  EGO CATO I. F. HELA I. HE ME \
✠────────────────────────────✠
```

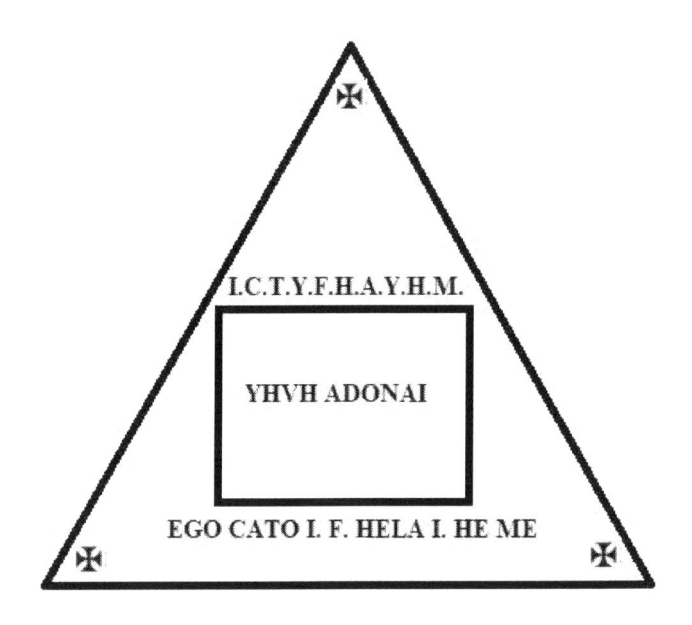

Make the above seal on clean parchment, consecrate it with the psalm, and hang it around the neck of the sick person.

Should you not be able to place it around the neck of the person; or if it is a long distance operation; write their name on the back of the seal and place it in your bible.

Pray the psalm daily for the person's health.

TO CALL THE DEAD

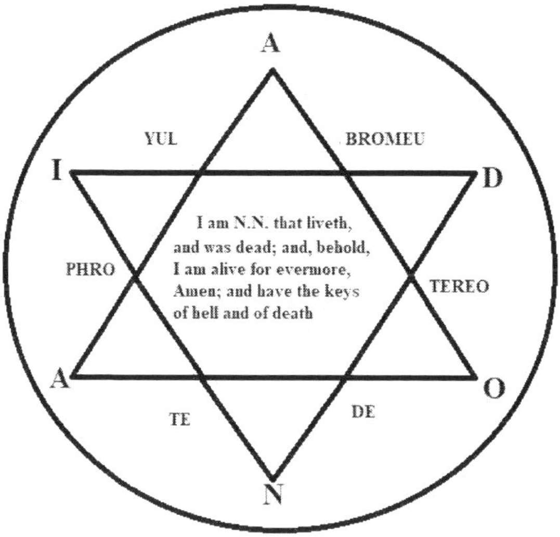
A
YUL
BROMEU
I
D
I am N.N. that liveth,
and was dead; and, behold,
I am alive for evermore,
Amen; and have the keys
of hell and of death
PHRO
TEREO
A
O
TE
DE
N

Mark the seal on clean paper with your own blood. Replace N.N. with the name of the shade you wish to call.

Wrap the seal in a stone of onyx and consecrate it with the psalm nine times. Place it under your pillow and pray the Lord's Prayer three times for the soul of the deceased.

To Calm Anger

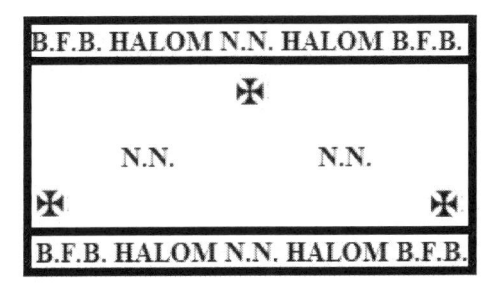

```
┌─────────────────────────────────────┐
│ B.F.B. HALOM N.N. HALOM B.F.B.      │
│                ✠                    │
│       N.N.          N.N.            │
│ ✠                              ✠    │
│ B.F.B. HALOM N.N. HALOM B.F.B.      │
└─────────────────────────────────────┘
```

Mark the above seal, and replace N.N. and N.N. with the names of the angry person, and the person who seeks forgiveness.

On the three crosses, burn three white candles and pray the psalm three times. Afterwards, give the seal to the person seeking forgiveness and have them place it under their pillow.

FOR FINANCIAL ASSISTANCE

> IOU TUM V.V. INDA IURE I. SACEM V. I.

Write the above names on clean paper and place them in an oil lamp. When you wake every day, night the lamp and recite the psalm.

PSALM 31

TO MAKE A PERSON SPEAK WITH YOU

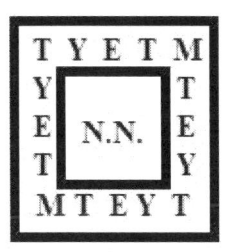

```
T Y E T M
Y       T
E  N.N. E
T       Y
  M T EY T
```

Mark the seal and replace N.N. with the person's name. Consecrate the seal with the Psalm, once a day for the intention of getting the person to speak to you. Carry the seal with you.

TO MAKE A PERSON'S FRIENDS LEAVE THEM

I.A.F.A.T.H.V.I.V.E.D.A.I.H.A.B.L.I.B.P.O.
I.A.F.A.T.H.V.I.V.E.D.A.I.H.A.B.L.I.B.P.O.
I.A.F.A.T.H.V.I.V.E.D.A.I.H.A.B.L.I.B.P.O.

Write the seal nine times on nine separate slips of paper. On the back, write the name of the person.

Every night at midnight for nine nights in a row, recite the psalm and burn the seal to ashes. Collect all the ashes together and mix with sulfur. Throw the ashes in the person's yard.

TO INVOKE PARANOIA AND DISCORD

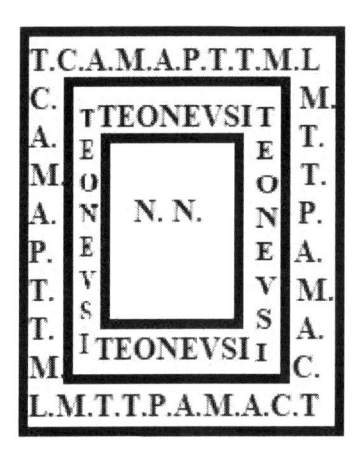

```
T.C.A.M.A.P.T.T.M.L
C.              M.
A.  TTEONEVSIT  T.
M.  E        E  T.
A.  O        O  P.
P.  N  N.N.  N  A.
T.  E        E  M.
T.  V        V  A.
M.  S        S  C.
    I TEONEVSI I
L.M.T.T.P.A.M.A.C.T
```

Mark the seal and replace N.N. with the name of the person. Wrap the seal around a lock of their hair, and place it within a glass bottle. Recite the psalm nine times into the bottle, and cork it. Seal the cork with wax, and throw the bottle over your left shoulder into a river or the ocean.

TO BE SAFE FROM INTRIGUE

```
        INI  TESET OYOPOYO

          YOHIHOY TEMET

            FAHIHAF
               A
               M
               E
               N
```

Pray the psalm seven times over the ink, and draw out the above seal. Carry this seal with you, should you be in danger of conspiracy and intrigue.

PSALM 32

TO OBTAIN FORGIVENESS

BITO✠VOTRA✠REFOR

Write the above names on clean paper, and place them in a bottle of pure olive oil. Recite the psalm over the oil, and anoint your head, throat, and heart with a cross. Repeat as needed.

TO HELP A PERSON GET OUT OF A CONTROLLING RELATIONSHIP

```
D.N.B.L.T.H.O.T.M.W.H.N.U.B.M.B.C.B.B.A.B
✠✠✠          N.N.              ✠✠✠
D.N.B.L.T.H.O.T.M.W.H.N.U.B.M.B.C.B.B.A.B
```

Mark the seal, and replace N.N. with the person's name. Pray the psalm over the seal daily, and keep it in your bible.

PROTECTION FROM FLOODS

```
SUTHE ROTHE MIVAV NORETEM
SUTHE ROTHE MIVAV RORETEM
SUTHE ROTHE MIVAV RORETEM
```

Pray the psalm and carry the seal around your property counterclockwise. Place the psalm outside above your door and rebuke the flood in the name of Jesus.

PSALM 33

TO MAKE A PERSON TELL THE TRUTH

```
F T W O
A I R A
T H I F
I A H D
```

Mark the seal and on the back write the person's name. Pray the psalm over it three times.

For distance working: Burn a purple candle over the seal while praying the psalm

For in person working: Burn the seal to ash, and mix it with the person's food.

TO DESTROY PLOTS AGAINST YOU

```
T.L.F.P.O.N.H.
L.           N.
F.           O.
P.   N N     P.
O.   ✠✠✠    F.
N.           L.
H.N.O.P.F.L.T.
```

Draw the seal on a heavy rock, replacing N.N. with the name of your enemy who plots against you. Everyday, turn the stone over and pray the psalm over it three times.

TO CATCH AN EVILDOER

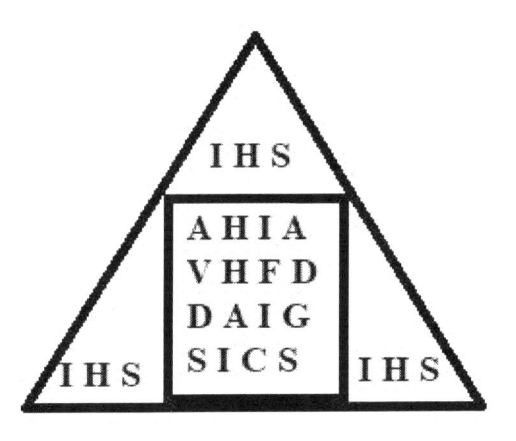

```
        I H S
      A H I A
      V H F D
      D A I G
 IHS  S I C S  IHS
```

Pray the psalm over the seal nine times, and place it in a jar. Seal the jar, and bury it facing the North.

PSALM 34

TO BE LOVED BY ALL

```
IWET
LAAT
HPWA
BOML
```

Mark the square, and the seal above it on the back, on a piece of copper, during the day and hour of Venus. Recite the psalm seven times, and fumigate the seal with rose and myrtle.

TO CALL AN ANGEL OF PROTECTION

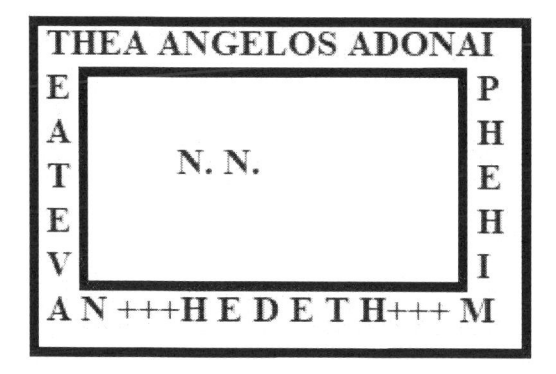

```
THEA ANGELOS ADONAI
E                        P
A                        H
T      N. N.             E
E                        H
V                        I
AN +++ H E D E T H +++ M
```

Mark the seal on clean parchment and replace N.N. with the person's name who you wish to protect.

Roll the seal into a small scroll and sew it up in a piece of red cloth. Pray the psalm over it three times in honor of the Most Holy Trinity, and give it to the person to wear around the neck.

TO PROTECT FROM SERIOUS INJURY

> HEPRA HIBO NOEO THEVI BEB
> HEPRA HIBO NOEO THEVI BEB
> HEPRA HIBO NOEO THEVI BEB

Pray the psalm seven times over ink and write the above words. Carry them on the person. When going out, pray the psalm and recite the words, crossing yourself three times.

PSALM 35

TO MAKE A PERSON MOVE

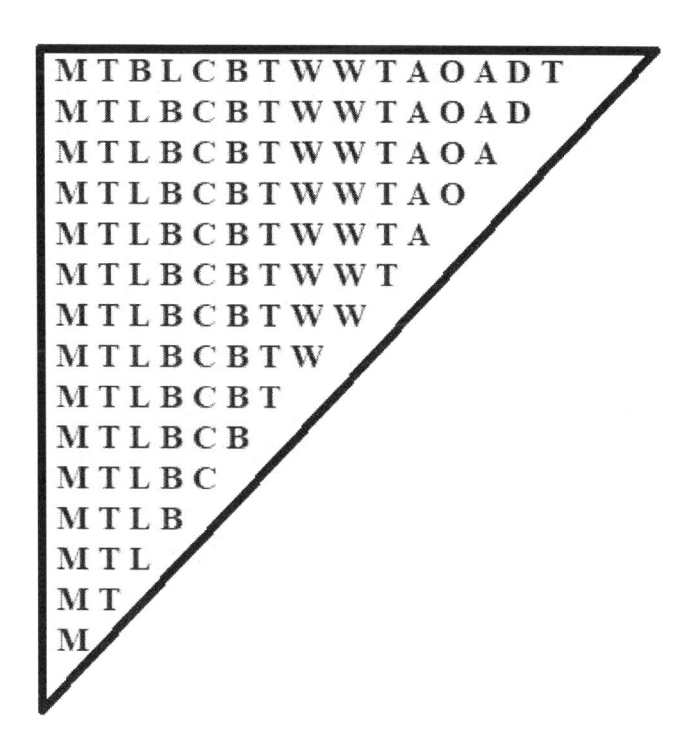

```
M T B L C B T W W T A O A D T
M T L B C B T W W T A O A D
M T L B C B T W W T A O A
M T L B C B T W W T A O
M T L B C B T W W T A
M T L B C B T W W T
M T L B C B T W W
M T L B C B T W
M T L B C B T
M T L B C B
M T L B C
M T L B
M T L
M T
M
```

Make the above seal, pray the psalm over it nine times, and hide it on the person's property or in their home.

Should this be impossible, make nine copies of the seal, praying the psalm once over each copy and burning it. Scatter the ashes where the person will walk over it.

TO BLOCK A PERSON'S LIFE

> **MATIR PEDARAD SERU TAO ADONAI PEM.**

On a Saturday during the hour of Saturn, write the above words on nine pieces of paper and pray the psalm over each one separately.

On the back, write the person's name on each seal.

Take the seals to the wilderness and dig a hole facing West. Read the seals one by one, dropping them in the hole. Cover the hole with a heavy rock.

TO SEND BACK A PERSON'S EVIL ACTIONS

```
M.T.N.T.H.E.T.
            X
M.T.F.I.T.P.
          N.N.
T.T.R
        T.T.R
N.N.
      M.T.F.T.P.
X
  M.T.N.T.H.E.T
```

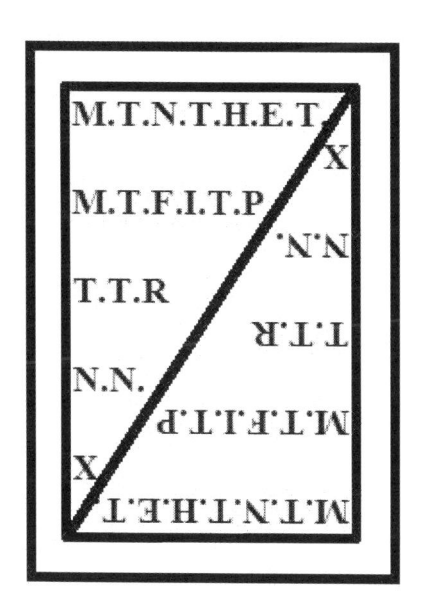

Write the above seal in black ink on the inside of a new bowl. During a lightning storm, pray the psalm three times in honor of the Most Holy Trinity, and leave the bowl outside to collect water. If possible, use India Ink or something similar, so the rain will dissolve the seal.

Take the water collected in the bowl and empty it at a crossroads or at the person's driveway, on their car, etc. The bowl is to be taken to a crossroads and shattered.

PSALM 36

TO GIVE A CHEATING SPOUSE A STD

```
E O T B
T P E T
C T T O
S C A Y
```

Mark the above square on a piece of the person's undergarments and pray the psalm seven times over it. Wrap the undergarments in a pig's foot and bury it in a drainage ditch.

TO INSURE FIDELITY

```
Yolodre Atothyofato Tes
Yolodre Atothyofato Tes
Yolodre Atothyofato Tes
       N.N.    N.N.
Yolodre Atothyofato Tes
Yolodre Atothyofato Tes
Yolodre Atothyofato Tes
```

Carry some of your hair and your partner's hair wrapped in the seal, written in your own blood.

Replace N.N. and N.N. with you and your partner's name and pray the psalm over it three times a day.

ADULTERY AND CHEATING

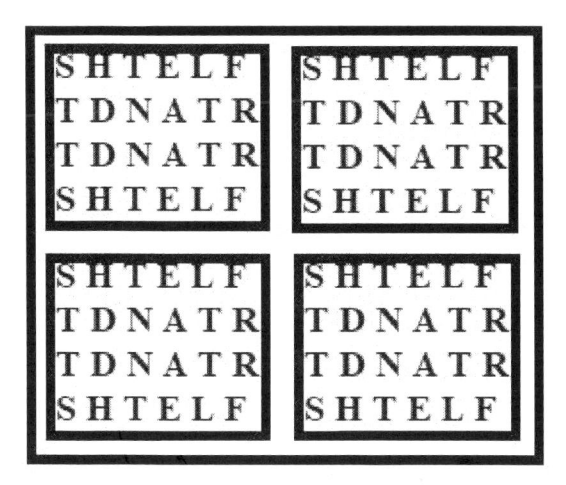

S H T E L F	S H T E L F
T D N A T R	T D N A T R
T D N A T R	T D N A T R
S H T E L F	S H T E L F
S H T E L F	S H T E L F
T D N A T R	T D N A T R
T D N A T R	T D N A T R
S H T E L F	S H T E L F

1. Make the seal on a piece of red cloth and take it to three Friday masses. Pray the psalm over it after each mass. Should you suspect your partner of cheating, when they are asleep, drag the cloth across their body. If they have cheated, they will have a fall and hurt themselves.
2. If your spouse has left you for another, and you wish to punish the adulterer, make the above seal on lead, and write the name of your ex-partner and their new partner on the back, using an iron nail to write the seal.

Drive the nail through the center of the seal, and dispose of it at a marketplace or busy intersection after praying the psalm 9 times over it.

PSALM 37

VINDICATION

```
            H W M Y
            R R S L
     I      T D Y V      H
            L T N S
H W M Y H W M Y H W M Y
R R S L R R S L R R S L
T D Y V T D Y V T D Y V
L T N S L T N S L T N S
            H W M Y
            R R S L
     H      T D Y V      V
            L T N S
```

Write the above seal on green cloth and pray the psalm over it seven times. Carry it hear your heart.

TO GET WHAT YOU ARE OWED

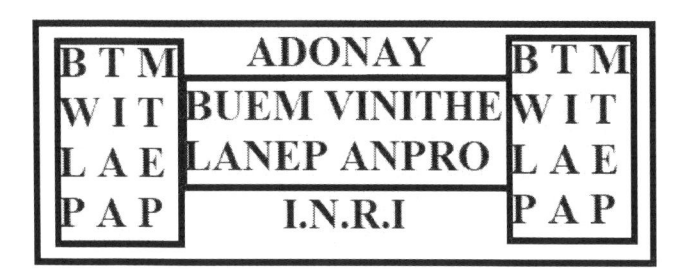

```
| B T M |   ADONAY      | B T M |
| W I T | BUEM VINITHE  | W I T |
| L A E | LANEP ANPRO   | L A E |
| P A P |   I.N.R.I     | P A P |
```

Mark the above seal in purple ink on a piece of birch bark. Pray the psalm over it 8 times and carry it with you.

TO EXPOSE THE WICKED

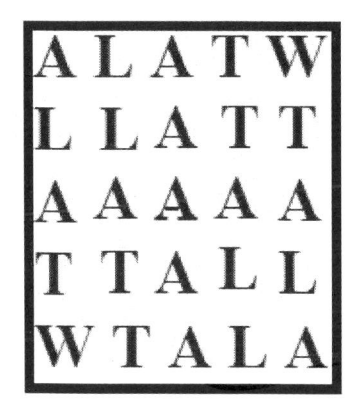

```
A L A T W
L L A T T
A A A A A
T T A L L
W T A L A
```

Mark the above seal on seven oak leaves, and the name of the evildoer on the back.

Recite the psalm seven times, burning one leaf each time. Do this in the open air, during the day.

PROTECTION FROM ASSAULT

```
B.T.S.W.P.T.O.H.A.T.B.W.B.B
B.T.S.W.P.T.O.H.A.T.B.W.B
B.T.S.W.P.T.O.H.A.T.B.W
B.T.S.W.P.T.O.H.A.T.B
B.T.S.W.P.T.O.H.A.T
B.T.S.W.P.T.O.H.A
B.T.S.W.P.T.O.H
B.T.S.W.P.T.O
B.T.S.W.P.T
B.T.S.W.P
B.T.S.W
B.T.S
B.T
B
```

Carry the above seal with you and recite the psalm three times over it before going out.

TO MAKE AN EVIL MAN LOSE ALL HE HAS

```
              BVHESO PA'AV NOMETI
                IHSAWARMFLALNT
                IHSAWARMFLALN
                IHSAWARMFLAL
                IHSAWARMFLA
                IHSAWARMFL
                IHSAWARMF
                IHSAWARM
   LOPHOR      IHSAWAR      HIHEC
                IHSAWA
                IHSAW
                IHSA
                IHS
                IH
                I
              UNOBEPH
```

Mark the above seal on metal with an iron nail, and the name of the evildoer on the back. When you wish to work the seal, pray the psalm over it three times and heat it in an oven.

Do this during the dark of the moon.

PSALM 38

FOR THE SICK AND INFIRM

ADONAY
D.N.F.M.D.N.B.F.F.M.M.
EL
C.Q.T.H.M.
ADONAI
SOTER

Recite the psalm over the seal six times and hang it about the person's neck.

PSALM 39

TO INVOKE POVERTY

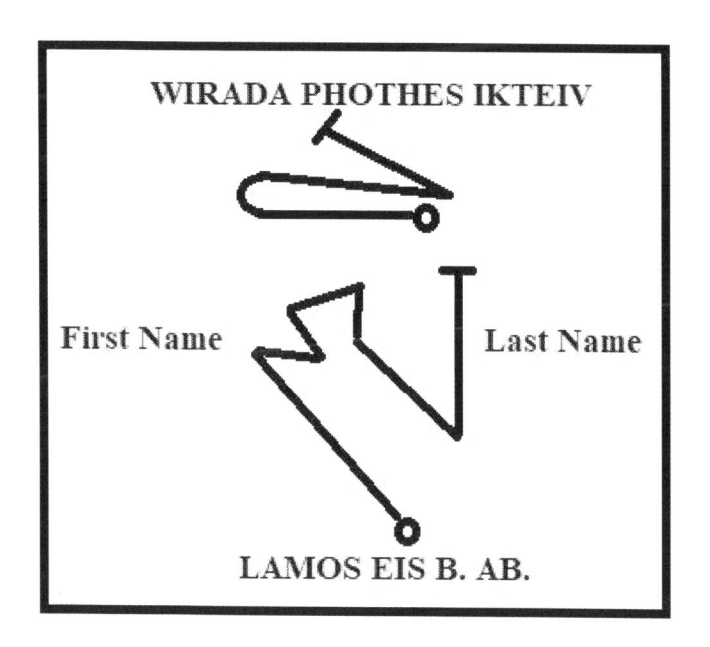

```
                WIRADA PHOTHES IKTEIV


First Name                              Last Name



                  LAMOS EIS B. AB.
```

On the day and hour of Saturn, make a tablet of beeswax and gravedirt and mark the above seal in it. Consecrate it by praying the psalm over it nine times.

The next Tuesday, fumigate the seal with peppercorns and throw the seal onto the person's roof before noon so the afternoon sun will melt the seal into their home.

TO SILENCE A WITNESS IN COURT

Mark the above seal with black ink over which you have chanted the psalm nine times. After each recitation, say **"N.N. Be still, be silent."**

Carry the seal with you to court.

PSALM 40

TO CHANGE BAD FORTUNE INTO GOOD FORTUNE

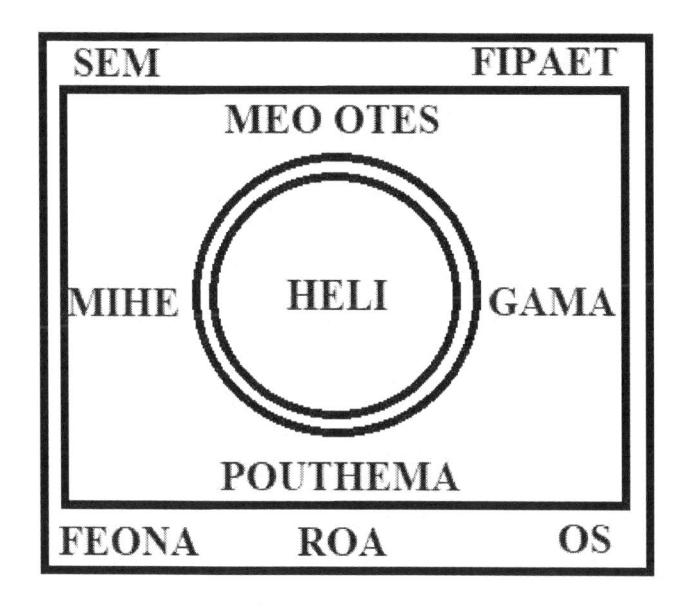

```
┌─────────────────────────────────────┐
│  SEM                      FIPAET    │
│      ┌─────────────────────────┐    │
│      │      MEO OTES           │    │
│      │       ╱─────╲           │    │
│      │      │       │          │    │
│  MIHE│      │ HELI  │    GAMA  │    │
│      │      │       │          │    │
│      │       ╲─────╱           │    │
│      │      POUTHEMA           │    │
│      └─────────────────────────┘    │
│  FEONA       ROA           OS       │
└─────────────────────────────────────┘
```

Carry the above seal on your person, near your heart. Everyday, cross yourself with the seal, and hold it in your right hand while you recite the psalm towards the South.

TO TURN SLANDER INTO PRAISE AND GOSSIP INTO HONOR

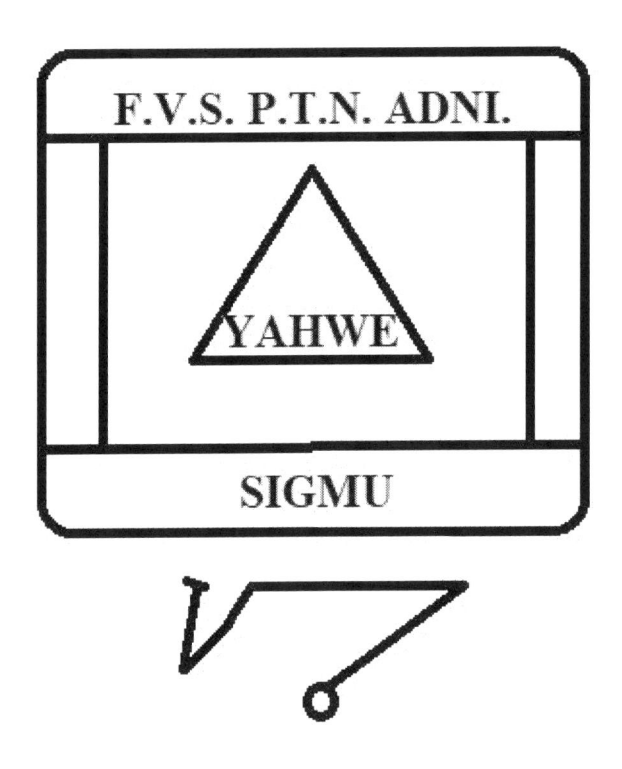

Pray the psalm thirty-three times over the ink and make the above seal. On the back, the sign below it. Fumigate it with frankincense.

TO MAKE YOUR HUSBAND OR WIFE RETURN

```
N.N. DET O. DOIOU LOGOS
┌───┬───┬───┐
│ I │ D │ T │
├───┼───┼───┤
│ Y │ W │ M │
├───┼───┼───┤
│ G │ L │ H │
└───┴───┴───┘
EL IOULA I.S. V.V. N.N. COR
```

Mark the above seal, replacing N.N. with the name of your spouse. Place this seal under your pattress and every night pray the psalm over your bed, facing the East.

TO CAUSE CONFUSION IN YOUR ENEMIES

MAL VV. VV. T.T. M. LIBE P.T.S. et COMAL V.V. DE M. RUBET BINDIS.

Submerge the above seal in the oil of an oil lamp and light it during the day and hour of Mercury while praying the psalm.

PSALM 41

TO TURN FRIENDS AGAINST ONE ANOTHER

E	M	C	F
S	I	T	O
W	S	M	B
H	T	A	M

Mark the above seal on dough and bake the bread. While the break is baking, pray the psalm nine times. Afterwards, split the break into two pieces and throw a piece in the yard of each of the persons you wish to turn against each other.

SO THE SICK WILL RISE FROM THEIR SICKBED

```
A S O  A S O  A S O
T E R  T E R  T E R
F R T  F R T  F R T
B O I  B O I  B O I
      ADONAY
A S O  A S O  A S O
T E R  T E R  T E R
F R T  F R T  F R T
B O I  B O I  B O I
```

Place the seal on the headboard daily, and pray the psalm three times, in honor of the Most Holy Trinity.

FOR DEER HUNTING

P	O	W	P
G	T	F	A
M	D	Y	F
S	S	S	M

Make the above seal on iron or deer parchment. Before going out to hunt, lay your ammunition upon the seal and recite the psalm seven times. Then carry the seal over your heart while hunting.

TO CAUSE DEPRESSION

```
M T H
B M F
D A N
```

Make the above seal on thin parchment and pray the psalm over it three times. Burn the seal to ashes and introduce it into the person's food or drink.

TO CAUSE ARTHRITIS

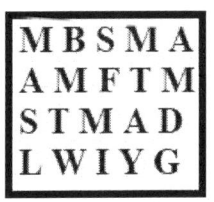

```
M B S M A
A M F T M
S T M A D
L W I Y G
```

N.N. B.S.M.A. N.N. B.S.M.A. N.N.

Make the square in ink fashioned from the ashes of burned chicken feathers mixed with tainted water. On the back, write the words, replacing N.N. with the person's name. Over this, pray the psalm for nine days. Then place the seal where the victim will walk over it.

PSALM 43

TO FIND FAVOR WITH JUDGES

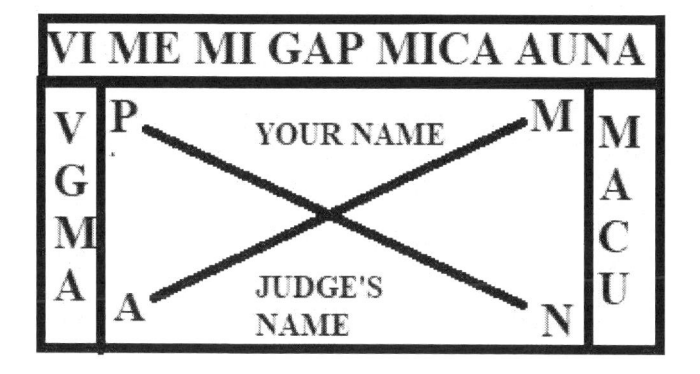

```
VI ME MI GAP MICA AUNA
V  P        YOUR NAME      M   M
G                              A
M                              C
A   A       JUDGE'S         N  U
            NAME
```

Carry the seal in both of your shoes and pray the psalm before entering the courtroom three times, in honor of the Most Holy Trinity.

TO RECEIVE AN ANSWER

```
              S.M. LUX et F.C.
        L                          L
        L                          B
        T                          P
        T                          M
        T                          M
        T                          W
             EL D.        T ZION
```

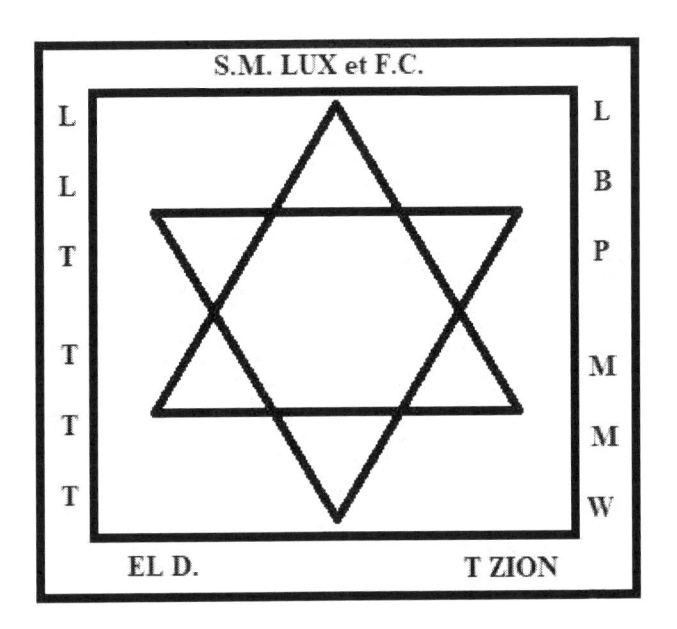

Mark the above seal, and write your question within the hexagram. While praying the psalm, burn the seal on myrrh incense.

PSALM 44

TO MAKE SOMEONE MOVE

```
W Y H Y D O T N
Y           T
H           O
Y           D
D           Y
O           H
T           Y
N T O D Y H Y W
```

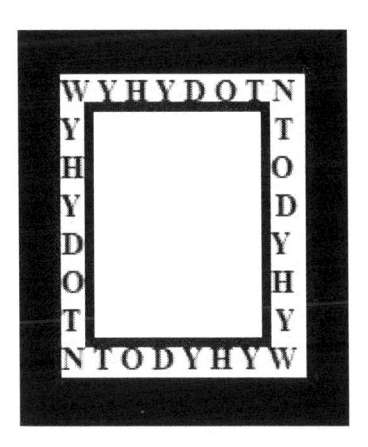

Make two copies of the seal. Write the name of the person in the center. Take dust or dirt from their yard and wrap one seal up with it and throw it over your left shoulder into a river after praying the psalm over it four times. The other seal, pray over four times, and place where they will walk over it.

TO DESTROY AN ENEMY

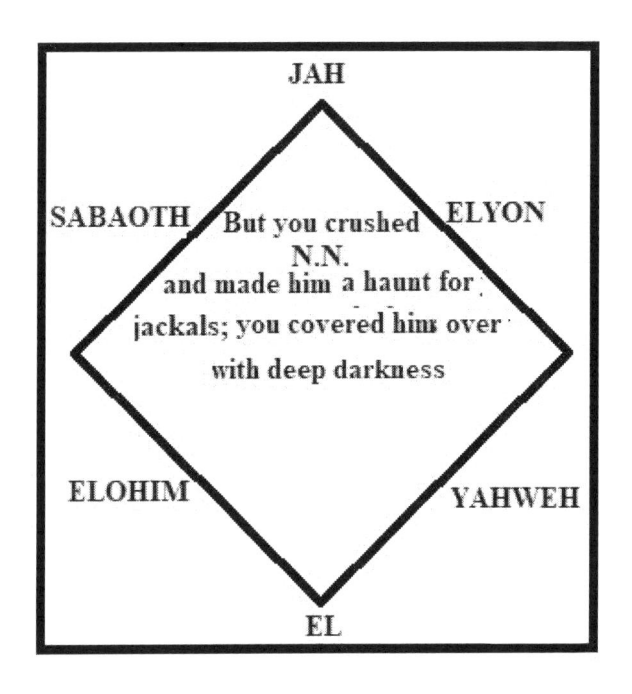

```
        JAH
         ◇
SABAOTH / But you crushed \ ELYON
        /      N.N.        \
       / and made him a haunt for \
      /  jackals; you covered him over \
     /       with deep darkness         \
ELOHIM                                YAHWEH
         \                          /
          \                        /
           \                      /
            \        EL          /
```

Mark the above seal on lead during the day and hour of Saturn, consecrating it with the psalm nine times. Bury it on the person's property. Replace N.N. with the person's name.

TO DEPRIVE A PERSON OF SLEEP AND REST

```
                A A W D Y S
                A         Y
                W         D
                D         W
                Y         A
A A W D Y S         A A W D Y S
A                             Y
W           N.N.              D
D                             W
Y                             A
S                             A
A A W D Y S         A A W D Y S
            A         A
            A         A
            W         W
            D         D
            Y         Y
            S         S
```

Mark the above seal on a piece of metal, and replace the tongue of a bell with it. Pray the psalm three times and ring the bell every night. The person will toss and turn and awaken as often as this is done.

PSALM 45

FOR A MAN TO ATTRACT WOMEN

```
G I S O
I S I M
O C I V
V S A M
```

Consecrate the seal seven times during the day and hour of Venus with the psalm on copper. Anoint it with rose oil and wear it near your genitals.

TO CAUSE PHYSICAL INJURY TO AN ENEMY

R	I	W	P
G	B	C	O
F	N	Y	H
E	T	A	S
L	M	K	U

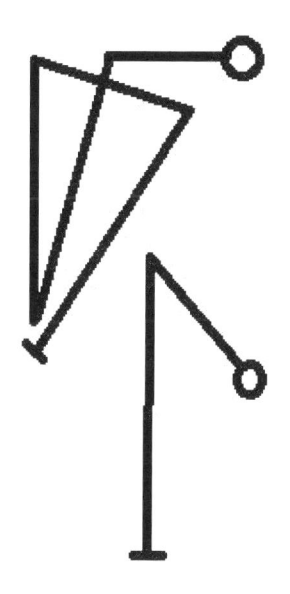

Mark the above square, with the signs on the back; on animal parchment. On the back, write the individual's name and pray the psalm five times over it. Place this on a tree, and shoot an arrow into it.

FOR A MAN TO FIND A WIFE

| DOCHARE AIHVAT IRHIST ROBING |

Pray the psalm daily and carry the above words with you, written on virgin parchment, and sewn up in green silk.

PSALM 46

TO REPAIR A RELATIONSHIP

> HEMAVV CETO EOTHEA
> HEMAVV CETO EOTHEA
> HEMAVV CETO EOTHEA
> N.N. ET N.N.
> HEMAVV CETO EOTHEA
> HEMAVV CETO EOTHEA
> HEMAVV CETO EOTHEA
> HEMAVV CETO EOTHEA

Mark the above seal in green ink on clean parchment, replacing N.N. et N.N. with your name and your partner's name. Place this under your mattress and pray the psalm over it daily, facing the East.

PSALM 47

FOR INHERITANCE ISSUES

```
         FUT     POYOV

      IE             HELO

          HECOUR
```

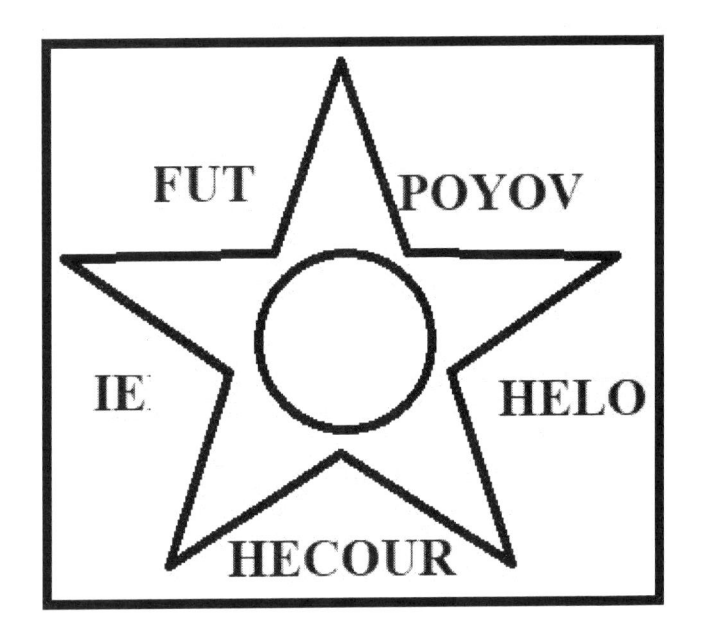

Make the seal on clean parchment, and within the circle write the name of the deceased. On the back, write your name and the name of your mother. Consecrate this seal eight times with the psalm and fumigate it with cinnamon.

PSALM 48

TO CAUSE A STORM AT SEA

```
      S
      O
      T
B A E WSY D T L
      T
      O
      S
```

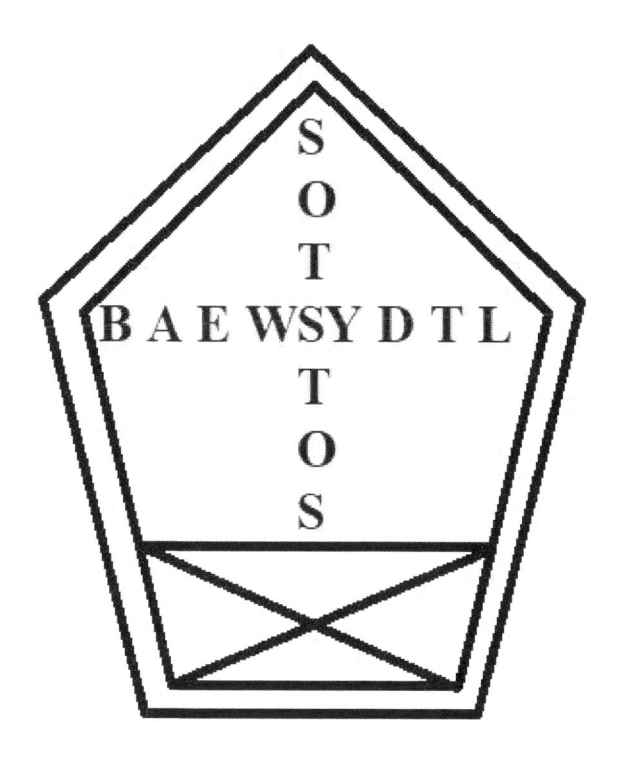

Mark the above seal on iron in the day and hour of Mars and consecrate it with the psalm, fumigating it with pig hair and peppercorns. Cast it into the sea over your left shoulder.

PSALM 49

IF A PERSON OR PLACE IS PLAGUED BY THE RESTLESS DEAD

```
T T V V R T H F
T T V V R T H
T T V V R T
T T V V R
T T V V
T T V
T T
T
```

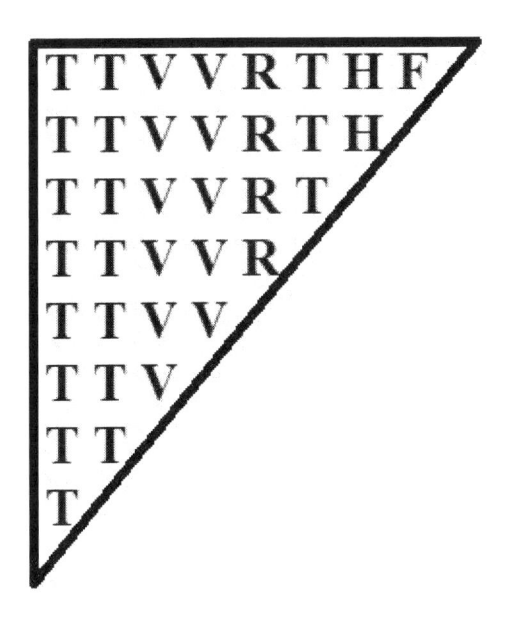

Take ink to a celebration of the Mass and hold it in your hand when the benediction is given. With that ink, make the above seal and consecrate it with the psalm nine times. Hang it from the person's neck, or place it hanging from a purple string in the center of the home that is plagued by ghosts.

PSALM 50

TO FIND WHAT IS LOST

> ADONAI ELOHIM GIBO S. ET S. H.A. F.T.R. OTSTO VVIS.

Write the above words on clean parchment and pray the psalm over them. Carry them with you, tied to your left wrist, and you will find what is lost.

TO BE FREE OF CRIMINAL CHARGES

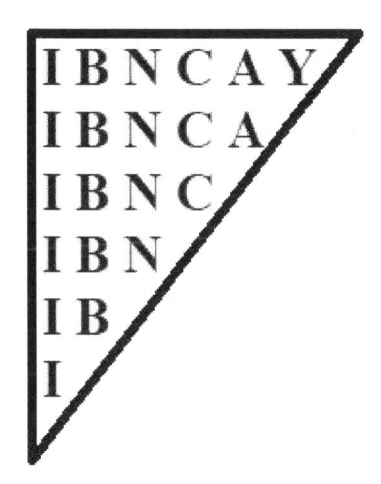

```
I B N C A Y
I B N C A
I B N C
I B N
I B
I
```

Mark the above seal on clean paper. Consecrate the seal with the psalm six times and swallow it.

TO CAUSE A PERSON TO BE BROUGHT UP ON CRIMINAL CHARGES

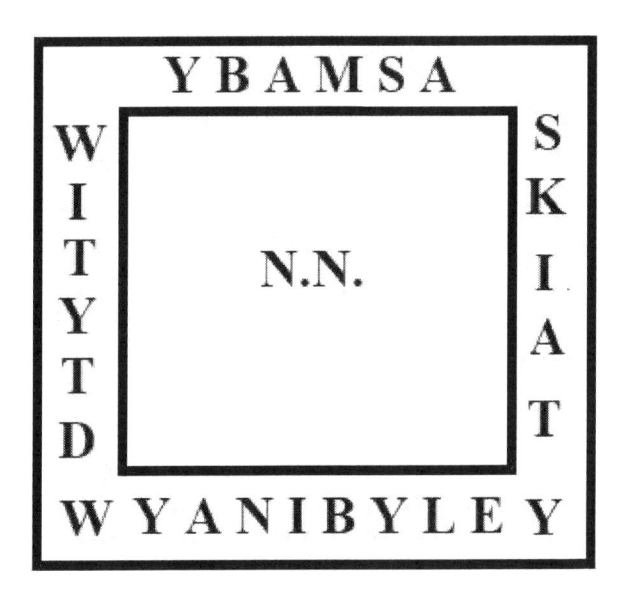

```
        Y B A M S A
W                         S
I                         K
T                         I
Y         N.N.            A
T                         T
D
        W Y A N I B Y L E Y
```

Mark the seal on lead, replacing N.N. with the person's name. Consecrate it with the psalm 9 times, and leave it in the grass at a police station.

FURTHER READING

Black and White Magic of Doctor Corbeaux Volume 1

A collection of spells, recipes, and workings based on the original classic "Black and White Magic of Marie Laveau." Includes the significance of cards in divination, the use of candles, psalms, roots, and oils

Black and White Magic of Dr. Corbeaux Volume 2

A collection of workings, spells, and recipes for various situations; modeled after the classic "Black and White Magic of Marie Laveau." Included in this volume are rituals with new saints, as well as a form of spider divination.

The Working Girl's Conjure Book: Hoodoo for Hookers

Everyone needs a little conjure in their lives and who more than the industrious working girl? Need protection while out on the job? Want a little something to strum up new business? Need a way to keep the police away? Want to tie down that really rich client? I've got a ritual for that…

SATOR AREPO TENET OPERA ROTAS: Prayers, Rituals, and Charms of Protection, Exorcism, and Uncrossing.

The following text presents a series of rituals, prayers, and charms for the purpose of protection, both physical and spiritual. The reversing of hexes, cleansing, and exorcism prayers will also be discussed.

Handy Human Finger Bones: Haintological Studies Volume 1

Handy Human Finger Bones: Haintological Studies is the first in a series of books where I will discuss subjects involving ghosts, graveyards, and the various beliefs and conjures relating to them. Over the course of these volumes, we will be discussing everything from power hotspots in cemeteries, how to conjure or expel the spirits of the dead, the materia magica of the graveyard, the occult significance of various human bones, and other folklore relating to the spirits of the dead in general.

Cartomancy 2.0: Further Studies in Cartomancy

In 2011 I wrote "Cartomancy; Divination with Playing Cards" (http://www.lulu.com/shop/dr-lazarus-corbeaux/cartomancy-divination-with-playing-cards/paperback/product-17990527.html) as an introductory bare bones extremely basic text on beginning divination with

54 playing cards. I was never really happy with my early books, and I have wanted to publish an update to my cartomancy book, with extended card meanings and spreads. To avoid repetitiveness, I will skip over the preliminary information that I have previously discussed in "Cartomancy; Divination with Playing Cards" and move directly on to the material I wish I had added in the original, as well as other helpful hints I never included in the original book. For those of you who have already read my previous book, you will be aware of the card correspondence regarding various saints and biblical events. In this text, I will include more correspondences, and include information on how the individual practitioner can graft the various spirits or deities they work with into the cards themselves.

Love Conjures: A Collection of Spiritual Works for Love and Relationships

What follows is a collection of recipes, workings, and advice to assist in the working of conjure for love, attraction, fidelity, and control for the use of individuals, both male and female, and of whatever sexual orientation. Before you make use of any of the herbs or materials referenced in this work, make sure you are not allergic. The key to success in conjuring a partner is to never get caught. Tell no one what you're doing, never let anyone see you doing it, and never admit to it. Often, though not always, should your target become aware of what you are doing, your works will falter - whether for psychological suggestion in the mind of the conjured, or through some esoteric principle inherent in love working, no one could say definitively. All I can say, it has been my experience that it is best to never let your target know that they are being, or have been conjured.

Santisima Muerte Trilogy: Altars, Prayers, and Rituals...with added materials

A trilogy of my original three books on the subject of the Santisima Muerte with added materials. Subjects included: how to erect an altar and work with the Santisima Muerte; recipes, rituals, and divination techniques to assist in communication with the saint.

Narco-Conjure Volume 1: Spells, Charms, and Formulas for Drug Dealers

What follows is a collection of prayers, charms, spells, rituals, formulas and folklore that may be of use to the purveyor of fine controlled substances for assistance in their economic endeavors. Need 5.0 off your back? Business too slow? Need some added protection on the street? Got a friend or employee in jail? Need to influence a court case? All this and more will be discussed

Black Magic for Kids: A Beginner's Guide to Hexes

There's no reason hexes, curses, and jinxes have to be complicated. Black Magic for Kids: A Beginner's Guide to Hexes presents a list of rituals, formulas, and prayers that are easily performed by the novice of all ages.

Black Magic for Kids Volume 2

Volume 2 of Black Magic for Kids contains the names, symbols, and rituals for employing the use of various evil spirits for practical purposes. Slightly more complex than Volume 1, but still an easy usable manual for the aspiring practitioner of the black arts.

Pum Pum Conjure: Attracting Women Through Conjure

A collection of charms, spells, and recipes for men to use for the sole purpose of attracting the romantic interests of ladies.

DIVINATION AND SPIRITUAL WORK

Copyright 2019 Dr. Corbeaux

If you would like to contact the author for divination or spiritual work, forward all questions to drcorbeaux@gmail.com

Author Page:
http://www.amazon.com/author/gedelazarus

Printed in Great Britain
by Amazon